THE PHILOSOPHY OF RABINDRANATH TAGORE

THE PHILOSOPHY OF RABINDRANATH TAGORE

S. RADHAKRISHNAN

GYAN

Published by

GYAN

Gyan Publishing House
5, Ansari Road
Daryaganj, New Delhi-110002
Phone: 011-47034999, 9811692060
E-mail: books@gyanbooks.com

Distribution Network
gyanbooks.com
India, USA, Canada, UK, Australia, France

ISBN: 978-81-212-9130-9 (PB)
First Published, 1919

2nd Impression 2023

Printed at: Gyan Press, Delhi.

THE PHILOSOPHY OF RABINDRANATH TAGORE
AUTHOR: S. RADHAKRISHNAN

THE PHILOSOPHY OF RABINDRANATH TAGORE

THE PHILOSOPHY OF RABINDRANATH TAGORE

BY

S. RADHAKRISHNAN

PROFESSOR OF PHILOSOPHY, MAHARAJAH'S COLLEGE, MYSORE

MACMILLAN AND CO., LIMITED
ST. MARTIN'S STREET, LONDON
1919

TO

SIR RABINDRANATH TAGORE

PREFACE

The book explains itself. The popularity of the writings of Sir Rabindranath Tagore shows that there is neither East nor West in the realm of spirit, and that his work meets a general want and satisfies a universal demand. What is the demand, and how it is met, are questions which I have tried to answer in this book.

In interpreting the philosophy and message of Sir Rabindranath Tagore, we are interpreting the Indian ideal of philosophy, religion, and art, of which his work is the outcome and expression. We do not know whether it is Rabindranath's own heart or the heart of India that is beating here. In his work, India finds the lost word she was seeking. The familiar truths of Hindu philosophy and religion, the value of which it has become fashionable to belittle even in the land of their birth, are here handled with such rare reverence and deep feeling that they seem to be almost new. My acquaintance with the soul of India from which Sir Rabindranath draws his inspiration has helped me in the work of exposition.

It may be said against this book that the author is trying to find a definite meaning where there is none, and is confusing his views with those of Sir Rabindranath. This charge raises a question too wide to discuss within the limits of a preface. But it must be remembered that Rabindranath writes poetry, while this book is in prose. Poetry is indefinite and suggestive, while prose is definite and expressive. What I have done here is simply to convert the vague suggestions of the poet into definite statements, supply the premises, draw out the conclusions, and give the setting where necessary. The book is an attempt to interpret Rabindranath's philosophy in the light of its own fundamental principles. I may here mention that the poet has been pleased to express his appreciation of this interpretation of his philosophy.

As the book would be lacking in wholeness without an account of Rabindranath's views about Nationalism in the East and the West, we have noticed his views on this subject in Chapters IV. and V., keeping literally close to his writings while giving an inward account of them.

It is the privilege of a preface to acknowledge obligations. I am very grateful to Sir Rabindranath Tagore for the permission given me to dedicate the book to him. Not to speak of the pleasure derived from association with such an honoured name, I seem to myself to repay in some degree the great obligation I owe him for having left a permanent impression on my mind, by inscribing this slender volume with his name. I am greatly indebted to Mr. C. F. Andrews of *Shantiniketan* for reading the proofs and making many valuable suggestions. My thanks are also due to the Editor of *The Quest* for granting me permission to use the two articles which originally appeared in his journal.

S. RADHAKRISHNAN.

MADRAS, *May* 27, 1918.

CONTENTS

CHAPTER I

PAGE

THE PHILOSOPHY OF RABINDRANATH TAGORE . . . 1

CHAPTER II

THE PHILOSOPHY OF RABINDRANATH TAGORE—II . 58

CHAPTER III

POETRY AND PHILOSOPHY 120

CHAPTER IV

THE MESSAGE OF RABINDRANATH TAGORE TO INDIA 172

CHAPTER V

THE MESSAGE OF RABINDRANATH TAGORE TO THE WORLD 254

CHAPTER I

THE PHILOSOPHY OF RABINDRANATH TAGORE

I

In vast life's unbounded tide
They alone content may gain
Who can good from ill divide
Or in ignorance abide—
All between is restless pain.
Before Thy prescience, power divine,
What is this idle sense of mine?
What all the learning of the schools?
What sages, priests, and pedants?—Fools!
The world is Thine, from Thee it rose
By Thee it ebbs, by Thee it flows.
Hence, worldly lore! By whom is wisdom shown?
The Eternal knows, knows all, and He alone.

OMAR.

"THE condemnation which a great man lays upon the world is to force it to explain him."[1] Rabindranath Tagore has not failed to force

[1] Hegel.

the world to come with its magazine articles and monographs to expound his views. The world-wide interest and popularity of his writings are due as much to the lofty idealism of his thoughts as to the literary grace and beauty of his writings. Rabindranath's teaching, with its vital faith in the redeeming power of the spiritual forces and their up-building energy, has a particular value at the present moment, when the civilised world is passing through the crucible of a ghastly war which, whether or not it purges the nations of their pride and hate, lust for gold and greed of land, at least proclaims, in no uncertain tones, the utter bankruptcy of materialism.

To be great is not merely to be talked about, it is also to be misunderstood, and Rabindranath has not escaped this fate. The many attempts made to explain him contradict each other, for "from the words of the poet men take what meanings please them." There are two views regarding his philosophy of life. If we believe one side, he is a Vedantin, a thinker who draws his inspiration from the Upanishads. If we believe the other, he is an advocate of a theism more or less like, if not identical with, Christianity. Rabindranath inclines to the former view. "To me the verses of the Upanishads and the teachings of Buddha have ever been things of the spirit, and therefore endowed with boundless vital growth; and I have used them, both in my own life and in my preaching, as being instinct with individual meaning for me, as for others, and awaiting for their confirmation my own special testimony, which must have its value because of its individuality."[1] Rabindranath's philosophy by life is viewed by this school as nothing but the ancient wisdom of India restated to meet the needs of modern times. His writings are a commentary on the Upanishads by an individual of this generation on whom the present age has had its influence. The soul of ancient India is mirrored in them. His idealism is a true child of India's own past and his philosophy is thoroughly Indian both in origin and development. In Dr. Coomaraswami's words, "the work of Rabindranath is essentially Indian in sentiment and form." The other view holds that Rabindranath Tagore, like other regenerators

[1] *Sādhanā*, p. 8.

of Hinduism, has freely borrowed from Christianity and Western teaching, and has woven these alien elements into the woof of his own faith. If he does not confess his indebtedness to the West, it is, in the words of the *Spectator's* reviewer, a case of "local patriotism," "ingratitude," and "insincerity."[1] "We have Mr. Tagore employing his remarkable literary talents in teaching borrowed Ethics to Europe as a thing characteristically Indian." "There is a fatal flaw of insincerity in its most seemingly elevated utterances."[2] These critics believe that the morals and philosophy underlying Rabindranath's thought are essentially Christian. They identify the Vedanta philosophy with a doctrine that makes the absolute an abstract beyond, the world an illusion, contemplation the way of escape, and extinction of soul the end of man. Obviously Rabindranath is not all this. He gives us a "human" God, dismisses with contempt the concept of the world-illusion, praises action overmuch and promises fulness of life to the religious soul. These are essentially the features of the Christian religion, and what is

[1] *Spectator*, February 14, 1914. [2] *Ibid.*

Rabindranath Tagore if not a typical Christian of the type spiritual India would produce in larger numbers in years to come? The Rev. Mr. Saunders remarks: "The God of *Gitanjali* is no impersonal, imperturbable absolute of Hindu philosophy, but in fact, whether He be explicitly Christ or not, He is at least a Christ-like God, and the experience of His suppliant and lover is one with the deep core of all Christian experience."[1] The Rev. Mr. Urquhart observes: "He opened his soul to the ideas of the West and he has drawn from Christianity, especially, ideas the influence of which upon his whole trend of thought has not always been acknowledged. The Eastern dress which he has given to these ideas has often concealed both from his own eyes and those of his readers their true origin, and although truth is one and inhabits no particular clime, absence of indication here has sometimes led to consequences prejudicial to the development of truth itself. The ideas of Rabindranath, like those of so many thinkers of modern India, have often been quite wrongly assigned to Indian

[1] *International Review of Missions*, 1914, p. 149.

sources."[1] Mr. Edward J. Thompson, who calls it "nonsense" to say that *Gitanjali* represents "true Hinduism," observes: "The man who henceforward must rank among the great religious poets of the world does not call himself a Christian: but in him we get a glimpse of what the Christianity of India will be like, and we see that it is something better than the Christianity which came to it."[2]

There is no use dogmatising at the very outset, for that would be to attack the central question at issue. An impartial exposition of Rabindranath's views would set at rest all doubts and disputes. We do not find any systematic exposition of his philosophy of life in any of his writings. Even *Sādhanā* is a book of sermons, or mystic hymns, or perhaps meditations. It is a sigh of the soul rather than a reasoned account of metaphysics; an atmosphere rather than a system of philosophy. But we feel that the atmosphere is charged with a particular vision of reality. In his writings we have the reaction of his soul to the environment, his attitude in the face of life.

[1] "The Philosophical Inheritance of Rabindranath Tagore," *International Journal of Ethics*, April 1916, p. 398.

[2] *Quarterly Review*, October 1914, p. 330.

His personality is completely revealed in his poems, which are the unconscious expression of his soul, the outpourings of his devotional heart, and the revelation of his poetic consciousness. His writings must and do contain suggestions of his intellectual creed. Though poetry is not philosophy, it is possible for us to derive from Rabindranath's works his philosophical views.

II

Human consciousness is the starting-point of all philosophic inquiry. The contradictions of human life provoke the quest for truth. Man is a finite-infinite being. He combines in himself spirit and nature. He is earth's child but heaven's heir. "At one pole of my being I am one with stocks and stones . . . . but at the other pole of my being I am separate from all."[1] As a link in the natural chain of events, man is subject to the law of necessity; as a member of the spiritual realm of ends, he is free. It is this contradiction, which we come across in science,

[1] *Sādhanā*, p. 69; see also *Fruit-Gathering*, XXXIII.

art, and morality, that demands a solution. The individual aspires after perfect truth, perfect beauty, and perfect goodness. But in the finite world he can only approximate to, but never completely possess, them. We can see the ideals as through a mist. Intellectually we aspire after an ideal of truth which is complete, harmonious, and all-comprehensive. The world of isolated facts is at best finite and conditioned. Intellect, with its separatist tendencies and dissecting habits, finds itself unable to grasp the whole. On the moral side, we feel the break between ideal aspirations and actual facts. There is a struggle between the infinite within, which makes the soul yearn for an ideal, and the lower finite, which is the heritage from the past evolution. "O Great Beyond, O the keen call of thy flute! I forget, I ever forget, that the gates are shut everywhere in the house where I dwell alone."[1]

There is a tension between the higher and the lower. The two elements have not attained a harmony. The higher self presents us with a moral imperative which we recognise

[1] *The Gardener*, 5; see also 6.

to be right, but our actual lower self contests its higher birth and pays homage to the delights of sense. This conflict is described in *Gitanjali*, 28.

Obstinate are the trammels, but my heart aches when I try to break them.

Freedom is all I want, but to hope for it I feel ashamed.

I am certain that priceless wealth is in thee, and that thou art my best friend, but I have not the heart to sweep away the tinsel that fills my room.

The shroud that covers me is a shroud of dust and death; I hate it, yet hug it in love.

My debts are large, my failures great, my shame secret and heavy; yet when I come to ask for my good, I quake in fear lest my prayer be granted.[1]

Even if we identify ourselves with the higher and fight the lower, it sometimes happens that we feel worsted. The natural forces seem too much for the moral. In this distress the finite individual asks: Is the moral

[1] These lines remind us of the classical passage in St. Augustine's *Confessions*: "Often does a man, when heavy sleepiness is on his limbs, defer to shake it off, and, though not approving, encourage it; even so was I sure it was better to surrender to thy love than to yield to my own lusts; yet though the former course convinced me, the latter pleased and held me back. There is nothing in me to answer thy call, 'Awake! thou sleeper,' but only drawling, drowsy words, 'Presently, yes, presently; wait a little while.' But the 'presently' had no present, and the 'little while' grew long, for I was afraid thou wouldst hear me too soon, and heal me at once of my disease of lust, which I wished to satiate rather than to see extinguished" (*Confessions*, xi.).

ideal a dream, and am I a fool to fight for it against the tremendous odds of nature? Have I a fighting chance of victory, or is the enterprise foredoomed to failure? Is the struggle between good and evil presided over by a higher Being on whom I could depend, or is it a great hazard where the result can be anything? As a rational being he craves for a working probability. So long as nothing definite is known, the finite soul, struck by the galling injustice and evil of the world, wrings his hands in despair and cries out to Heaven: What must I do to be saved? Wretched man that I am, who shall deliver me from the body of this death? The contradictions of finite life clearly establish that the finite individual is not the ultimate in the world but only an incomplete something requiring supplementation. The need for a philosophy which would reconcile the opposing elements of life, self and not-self, is felt to be urgent.

III

If what our intellect reveals to us is true, if the world is a chance congeries of individuals attempting without success to fight and conquer nature, the best thing for the wise man would be to withdraw from the universe and contemplate the noble ideals in his cloister, leaving the world to rack and ruin. Mr. Bertrand Russell represents this tendency very forcibly in his brilliant article on "The Free Man's Worship": "That man is the product of causes which had no prevision of the end they were achieving; that his origin, his growth, his hopes and fears, his loves and his beliefs are but the outcome of accidental collocations of atoms; that no fire, no heroism, no intensity of thought and feeling can preserve an individual life beyond the grave; that all the labours of the ages, all the devotion, all the inspiration, all the noonday brightness of human genius, are destined to extinction in the vast depth of the solar system, and that the whole temple of Man's achievement must inevitably be buried beneath the debris of a universe in ruins,—all these things, if not quite beyond dispute, are yet so nearly certain that no philosophy which rejects them can hope to stand."[1] "Blind to good and evil, reckless of

[1] *Philosophical Essays*, pp. 60-61.

destruction, omnipotent matter rolls on its relentless way."[1] Spiritual tempers recognise the high worth of human aspirations and require of men a contemplation of the ideals sacred to humanity. The way to escape from the sway of fate lies in giving up the ties binding man to the external world. We are exhorted by Mr. Russell "to abandon the struggle for private happiness, to expel all eagerness of temporary desire, to burn with passion for eternal things. This is emancipation, this is Free Man's Worship."[2] The pessimists of all ages demand an extirpation of desires and an attainment of inner freedom. The world is full of contradictions and human life is a great discord. The external world appears to be so awry that it drives man into the deepest solitudes of the soul. A sort of other-worldly mysticism which treats with contempt both nature and man develops. The Absolute is said to be quite different from the world, just the opposite of the finite. The characteristics we are acquainted with in the finite universe can only be denied of it. It alone is real and the world is unreal. Such

[1] *Philosophical Essays*, p. 70. [2] *Ibid.* p. 69.

an intellectualist philosophy will make the Absolute an abstract beyond, the world an unreality, contemplation the way of escape, and extinction of soul the end of man. But the Absolute will then be left in a perilous state, having nothing to do with the universe. This view is a confession of the defeat or discomfiture of man and can never satisfy his real needs. In this conflict of forces, self and not-self, right and might, there are thinkers who ask us to take up sides with might and wickedness. Nietzsche demands worship of force. The God of earth is a God of might and vengeance and not a God of right and conscience. This view is so patently absurd that we need not waste words over it.

A different view, meant especially to emphasise the religious needs of man, prevails in the West. According to it self and not-self are opposed. "The West seems to take a pride in thinking that it is subduing nature, as if we are living in a hostile world where we have to wrest everything we want from an unwilling and alien arrangement of things."[1]

[1] *Sādhanā*, p. 5. Professor Baillie, of Aberdeen, concurs with this view, and thinks that the characteristic differences in mentality between

The world of nature is regarded as a refractory force hard in resisting and slow in giving in. Man in his battlings with matter presided over by Satan requires the help of God. God along with mankind struggles to overcome the forces of evil and darkness. All such theistic conceptions generally end in making God a finite being. Leibnitz, in his famous *Theodicy*, makes God a limited one. He says the existing world is the best of all possible worlds. Evidently all worlds were not possible to God; He selected the best possible, and it has turned out to be not quite a good one. Mill holds to a limited God in his *Essay on Religion*. Doctors James, Schiller, and Rashdall postulate a finite and personal God. These thinkers hold to a

---

religious Asia and scientific Europe can be traced ultimately to this difference in view regarding man and environment. He writes: "The scientific movement arises from a peculiar attitude of the mind to the world found amongst certain peoples of the globe, and without this attitude science will always appear a curiosity or an irrelevance. The attitude may be shortly described as due to a sense of the detachment of man from the world as something alien and external, to a sense of the supremacy of his aims over the process of the outer nature. In the East man seems to feel no sense of alienation; he seems to feel himself as much a part of the universe as a plant is inseparable from its environment. So much is this the case that man's life is felt to be part of the very current of the stream of the vaster life of the world" (*Hibbert Journal*, April 1917, p. 363).

pluralistic conception of the universe and find themselves unable to account for the unity of the world-process. No religion can finally rest in a God who is engaged in a conflict with evil in which He requires the help of man. We can never be sure of the outcome of the struggle. It is quite possible that a God who is limited by the resisting evil may have, like man, defeat for His end; only, if man fails with the help of God, great is his fall indeed. The defeat is more fearful when God has not deserted the side on which man is. A suffering God, a deity with a crown of thorns, cannot satisfy the religious soul. He is one among many, subject to the limitations of man. There is a great gulf fixed between humanity presided over by God and nature led by His opposite. So long as one principle has not universal sway, so long the basis of pessimism is sound and safe. How can man, without the joy of hope and confidence in victory, bear up against the pressure of alien force? The fear of what the unknown and the unknowable energy might do fills his life with doubt and misery, weakness and distraction. Only a universal principle can deliver human life from despair. The

Absolute is nothing short of the universe in its totality. It is the whole of perfection in which the opposition of good and evil is overcome. But the theist's God is identified with a part of the universe, the good, while the evil is left in its own independence. God is the virtue of the virtuous, and there is another opposing Him, the wickedness of the wicked. The God of theism is only an aspect of the Absolute, an appearance of a deeper reality. Modern theism, aware of this difficulty, lays stress on Divine immanence, thus watering down the personal God into the Absolute whole.[1] The views here referred to "read the world wrong" and do not give us a philosophic synthesis of God, world and self, for in a true synthesis we cannot have absolute divisions between man and nature. We need a principle, superior to them all, which would assign to each, self and not-self, its appropriate value, and give harmony to their mutual relations; a principle of synthesis which would comprehend both elements and transform their apparent antagonism into an organic relationship.

[1] See Dr. Campbell, *New Theology*, and *Foundations*, by Oxford thinkers, especially Dr. Moberly's essays.

A closer scrutiny reveals to us the kinship of nature and spirit, not-self and self. The fact that we are able to interpret nature, know it, appreciate it, fight and conquer it, shows that it is akin to human consciousness: "We could have no communication whatever with our surroundings if they were absolutely foreign to us." Man is "reaping success every day, and that shows there is a rational connection between him and nature, for we never can make anything our own except that which is truly related to us." If we separate man from nature "it is like dividing the bud and the blossom into two separate categories, and putting their grace to the credit of two different and antithetical principles." "The Indian mind never has any hesitation in acknowledging its kinship with nature, its unbroken relation with all."[1] In India where civilisation developed in forests near to nature, there was no thought of an antagonism between man and nature, no idea of forcibly wresting treasures from nature.

Human consciousness, animal life, and inanimate nature are different grades of the

[1] *Sādhanā*, pp. 5-7.

same energy, stages of the same development. Self and not-self into which the universe has been dichotomised are no rivals, but are the different expressions of the same Absolute, different modes of its existence. Nature is not antagonistic to spirit; not-self is there for the purpose of being used up by the spirit. It is fuel for the flame of the spirit. The Taittiriya Upanishad calls matter *annam* or food. The human will converts its environment into food. Objective nature is capable of being determined in accordance with the subject's wishes. The past progress of the Universe clearly establishes the success which has attended man's attempt to utilise the environment for the ends of life and spirit. The not-self is a means for the manifestation of spiritual power. Only through nature can spirit realise itself. "The earth, water and light, fruits and flowers, to her were not merely physical phenomena to be turned to use and then left aside. They were necessary to her in the attainment of the ideal of perfection, as every note is necessary to the completeness of the symphony."[1] If we adopt the right attitude

[1] *Sādhanā*, p. 7.

to nature, we feel the pulse of spirit throbbing through it. A true seer sees in natural facts spiritual significance. The poetic temper hears the voice of spirit crying aloud in nature. "The man whose acquaintance with the world does not lead him deeper than science leads him, will never understand what it is that the man with the spiritual vision finds in these natural phenomena. The water does not merely cleanse his limbs, but it purifies his heart; for it touches his soul. The earth does not merely hold his body, but it gladdens his mind; for its contact is more than a physical contact, it is a living presence. When a man does not realise his kinship with the world, he lives in a prison-house whose walls are alien to him. When he meets the eternal spirit in all objects, then is he emancipated, for then he discovers the fullest significance of the world into which he is born; then he finds himself in perfect truth, and his harmony with the All is established."[1] The eye of an artist is needed to perceive the spiritual beauty of the things of nature. Only his eye can penetrate through the confusing

[1] *Sādhanā*, p. 8.

chaos of shadows and appearances, and see the cosmos within. Rabindranath has the eye which pierces into the secret of which the natural fact is the sign and prophecy. He is a poet of nature in whose hands the crudest stuff of existence acquires a poetic colouring. The spiritual phases of nature leap up to his God-filled eyes, kindle devotion in his heart, and set song on his lips. To his soul touched by God the physical world of science appears in all its sweetness and simplicity as to a child. It is a "fairy universe where the stars talk and the sky stoops down to amuse him, and all nature comes to his window with trays of bright toys."[1] To him "the touch of an infinite mystery passes over the trivial and the familiar, making it break out into ineffable music." "The trees, the stars, and the blue hills" ache "with a meaning which can never be uttered in words."[2] A breath of divine passion passes over the whole world, making it pure and perfect. He feels "a thrill passing through the air with the notes of the far-away song floating from the other shore."[3] He can

[1] See "Baby's World" in *The Crescent Moon*.

[2] *Sādhanā*, p. 43.

[3] *Gitanjali*, 21.

never escape the divine presence, twist and turn as he will. The deep shadows of the rainy July and the stormy night suggest God's presence. He is a mystic soul who can hear the voice of God in the tempest and see His hand in the stilling of the wave.

It is no wonder that Rabindranath advocates life in nature and in the open as the best means of spiritual progress, for in nature the religious eye will see the infinite lying stretched in silent smiling repose. Rabindranath sings not of the cloister or the retreat, but of the open highway and the King's Post Office. He revels in the open air and is not afraid to stand under the golden canopy. According to him the best way to derive divine inspiration is to lose oneself in the contemplation of nature. In silence and in solitude we have to enjoy the presence of the divine in nature.

> I woke and found his letter with the morning.
>
> When the night grows still and stars come out one by one I will spread it on my lap and stay silent.
>
> The rustling leaves will read it aloud to me, the rushing stream will chant it, and the seven wise stars will sing it to me from the sky.[1]

---

[1] *Fruit-Gathering* IV ; see also XV. and LXVIII.

He does not lay stress on religious instruction in the Bolpur school, but believes that religious feeling and piety will work their way into the life of the students if the environment is pure and noble. "We do not want nowadays temples of worship and outward rites and ceremonies. What we really want is an *Asram*. We want a place where the beauty of nature and the noblest pursuits of man are in a sweet harmony. Our temple of worship is there where outward nature and human soul meet in union." Recognising the influence of environment upon temperament, the ancient teachers chose the forest shades or the banks of holy rivers as the sites for their Asrams. When we are filled with the sense of the divinity that surrounds us, then we feel impelled to give ourselves up to reverie or meditation on God.

> To-day the summer has come at my window with its sighs and murmurs; and the bees are plying their minstrelsy at the court of their flowering grove.
>
> Now it is time to sit quiet, face to face with thee, and to sing dedication of life in this silent and overflowing leisure.[1]

---

[1] *Gitanjali*, 5.

Again:

> In the busy moments of the noontide work I am with the crowd, but on this dark lonely day it is only for thee that I hope.
>
> If thou showest me not thy face, if thou leavest me wholly aside, I know not how I am to pass these long rainy hours.[1]

In moments of such exaltation when we silently adore the living presence that reveals itself through the grandeur of nature, which makes itself heard in the soul through the contemplation of the world of immanent divinity, a great peace steals over us. The infinite then murmurs its secret into our ears, and tells the story of the soul and the legend of the earth. To commune with the unutterable, we should get away from the noisy world of action, escape from the machinery of life which kills the soul. Dull mechanical work degrades and brutalises the individual, while a life of nature elevates and purifies the soul. Rabindranath beautifully depicts how an enthusiastic surrender to the spontaneity of natural scenery leads a man to his goal.

> I laid myself down by the water and stretched my tired limbs on the grass.

---

[1] *Gitanjali*, 18.

My companions laughed at me in scorn. They held their heads high and hurried on; they never looked back nor rested; they vanished in the distant blue haze. They crossed many meadows and hills, and passed through strange, far-away countries. All honour to you, heroic host of the interminable path! Mockery and reproach pricked me to rise, but found no response in me. I gave myself up for lost in the depth of a glad humiliation—in the shadow of a dim delight.

At last, when I woke from my slumber and opened my eyes, I saw thee standing by me, flooding my sleep with thy smile.[1]

We then lie exposed to all the winds of heaven that blow. We feel a presence, all love and peace. The load slips off our heart, and the soul is lifted above life, petty, vexatious, and harassing, and slides into a perfect harmony. The divine light floods the soul, the divine music ravishes it, and the soul expresses its joy by humming the hymn of the universe. So running "upon the dusty path of the despised" takes us nearer to God.[2] In *The Post Office*, the child Amal, rid of the prejudices of the sophisticated Madhav, wistfully yearns to get away from the clank of crowds, the noise and glare of the town, into countryside with its hills and dales. Even though his

[1] *Gitanjali*, 48. [2] *Fruit-Gathering*, X.

continuance in the world is said to depend on his keeping indoors, the cage bird longs to be a free bird and enjoy the freedom of the woodland. For as it is put in *The Cycle of Spring*: "This outer world has been made with a lavish expenditure of sun and moon and stars. Let us enjoy it, and then we can save God's face for indulging in such extravagance."[1]

Rabindranath's conception of nature is antagonistic to the view which makes nature opposed to the self and its aspirations. He has a positive view of the relation of spirit to nature. The two are aspects of the Absolute. Nature and society are revelations of the divine spirit. The same light dwells in the world outside and the world within. This ultimate oneness of things is what the Hindu is required to remember every moment of his life. "The text of our everyday meditation is the *Gayatri*, a verse which is considered to be the epitome of all the Vedas. By its help we try to realise the essential unity of the world with the conscious soul of man; we learn to perceive the unity held together by the one Eternal Spirit, whose power creates the earth,

[1] Page 51.

the sky, and the stars, and at the same time irradiates our minds with the light of a consciousness that moves and exists in unbroken continuity with the outer world."[1] The song of the soul and the music of the spheres are but the expressions of the divine harmony.

> The same stream of life that runs through my veins night and day runs through the world and dances in rhythmic measures.[2]

The same spirit dwells in the most distant sun and in the darkest depths of the soul. Nature is not a hostile power harassing man at every turn; the universe is not foreign to us.

> When in the morning I looked upon the light I felt in a moment that I was no stranger in this world.[3]

Rabindranath's conception of the unity of the world gives us the assurance that the ideals of Science and Morality are real, and sustains us on the path of right untempered by the grim realities of pain and crime. It makes us realise how the spiritual forces of the world co-operate with us in our endeavours. If the distinction of man and world, self and not-self, were the last thing,

[1] *Sādhanā*, p. 9. [2] *Gitanjali*, 69. [3] *Ibid* 95.

then "there would have been absolute misery and unmitigated evil in this world. Then from untruth we never could reach truth, and from sin we never could hope to attain purity of heart; then all opposites would ever remain opposites, and we could never find a medium through which our differences could ever tend to meet."[1] Then our life would become a hideous tragedy of waste and wrong, fear and weakness. But progress in the realms of Science, Art, and Morality shows that self and not-self are only relatively opposed. It is the business of man to break down the opposition, and make both express the one spirit. This view restores the balance between nature and spirit, and makes life worth living. "It were well to die if there be Gods, and sad to live if there be none."[2] If there is the all-embracing spirit, the glooms and shadows of life lose their edge and bitterness. Then we feel that we are not battling with an unknown antagonist on a doubtful issue, but that we are trying to realise progressively a victory that is guaranteed to us. Perfect confidence takes the place of blank despair. The confused and

[1] *Sādhanā*, p. 105.

[2] Marcus Antoninus.

shadowy world of experience becomes quite clear and transparent. Doubt is vanquished; the contradictions of life cease. "All that is harsh and dissonant melts into one sweet harmony."[1]

IV

The creation of the universe is only the realisation of the Absolute, the revelation of its freedom. "God finds himself by creating."[2] It is the creative joy that gives birth to the universe, which is not only separate from God but also united to Him. God is the basis of the whole universe. It is the self-sundering of the Eternal which calls into existence the universe of men and things. But this must have "duality for its realisation."[3] The whole breaks up its individuality into the two aspects of self and not-self, Iswara and Maya, Purusha and Prakriti. "When the singer has his inspiration he makes himself into two; he has within him his other self as the hearer, and the outside audience is merely an extension of this other self of his. The lover seeks his own other self in his beloved. It is the joy that

[1] *Gitanjali*, 2. [2] *Stray Birds*, 46. [3] *Sādhanā*, p. 104.

creates this separation, in order to realise through obstacles the union."[1] The not-self or Prakriti or Maya is generally conceived of as the passive and the self as the active principle. It is their mutual supplementation that promotes the unity of the universe. The Eternal One realises itself by the action and interaction of the two principles. The principle of negativity impels the Eternal One to realise itself in the world. It is the woman "in the heart of creation." "She who is ever returning to God his own outflowing of sweetness; she is the ever fresh beauty and youth in nature; she dances in the bubbling streams and sings in the morning light; she with heaving waves suckles the thirsty earth; in her the Eternal One breaks in two in a joy that no longer may contain itself, and overflows in the pain of love."[2] The first existent out of the Absolute is Iswara with the not-self over against him. Iswara is the personal God who represents the ideal of goodness to the finite minds. He is the father, creator or governor of the universe. The not-self is the negative reflection of the affirmative Iswara. The whole universe

[1] *Sādhanā*, p. 104. [2] *Fruit-Gathering*, LVI.

develops in, through, and by means of, the interaction between these two.

> Whatever being is born, the unmoving or the moving, know thou, O best of the Bharathas, that to be owing to the union of Kshetra and Kshetragnya (matter and spirit, finite and infinite).[1]

> Between the poles of the conscious and the unconscious, there has the mind made a swing:
> Thereon hang all beings and all worlds, and that swing never ceases its sway.
> Millions of beings are there: the sun and the moon in their courses are there:
> Millions of ages pass, and the swing goes on.
> All swing! the sky and the earth and the air and the water; and the Lord Himself taking form:
> And the sight of this has made Kabir a servant.[2]

The universe is the eternal sacrifice of the supreme. The Bhagavadgita says: "The whole world rests on sacrifice. It is the law of the universe."[3] He is sacrificing himself that nature and humanity may live. This self-sundering of the whole in which the world is contained is but the expression of his joy and the law of the universe. It is "the joy that makes the earth flow over in the riotous excess of the grass, the joy that sets the twin brothers,

[1] Bhagavadgita, XIII. 16.

[2] *Kabir's Poems*, XVI.

[3] III. 14.

life and death, dancing over the wide world, the joy that sweeps in with the tempest, shaking and waking all life with laughter, the joy that sits still with its tears on the open red lotus of pain, and the joy that throws everything it has upon the dust, and knows not a word."[1] The outburst of joy is needed for the realisation of the concrete richness of the world. The universe is new-born continually, as a result of this joy.

> This frail vessel thou emptiest again and again, and fillest it ever with fresh life.[2]

This lesson that "the old is ever new" is the central theme of *The Cycle of Spring.*[3] The Absolute realises through separation and union.

> The child finds its mother when it leaves her womb.
> When I am parted from you, thrown out from your household, I am free to see your face.[4]

This separation is needed to make the eternal concrete.

> You did not know yourself when you dwelt alone. I came and you woke.[5]

---

[1] *Gitanjali*, 58. [2] *Ibid.* I.
[3] Page 35. [4] *Fruit-Gathering*, X.
[5] *Ibid.* LXXX.

Thou settest a barrier in thine own being and then callest thy severed self in myriad notes. This thy self-separation has taken body in me.

The great pageant of thee and me has overspread the sky. With the tune of thee and me all the air is vibrant, and all ages pass with the hiding and seeking of thee and me.[1]

It is the pang of separation that spreads throughout the world and gives birth to shapes innumerable in the infinite sky.[2]

But the separation of the two is not the last word. The universe is not merely a going forth from God, but is also a coming towards Him. The union of the two is complete, but in the universe it is being made. The finite represents to us the tension of the self to become the infinite. The universe is the struggle of the finite to reach the infinite. It is a play of hide and seek between the two, God and man. All objects of the world are finite-infinite, but the tension between the two is at its highest in the human consciousness. Man approximates to the ideal but never *qua* man reaches it. The world is the process of becoming infinite, but not the consummation. Should man completely realise the infinite, and should the world reach its goal of becoming

[1] *Gitanjali*, 71. [2] *Ibid.* 64.

the infinite, then there will be no universe and necessarily no Absolute.

> O thou lord of all heavens, where would be thy love if I were not?[1]

Though God is everything, everything is not God. While the whole universe is regarded by Rabindranath as the expression of God, still different things express God in different degrees. He thus admits the conception of degrees of reality. "The revealment of the infinite in the finite, which is the motive of all creation, is not seen in its perfection in the starry heavens, in the beauty of the flowers. It is in the soul of man."[2] Man, the animal with the upward look, is a higher revealment than the mere animal, and the animal is higher than the worm, which is higher than the clod. "To all things else you give; from me you ask."[3] Subject to this reservation we can say that the objects of the universe are parts of God aspiring to be the whole. God is the infinite ideal of perfection. Man has yet to become what he is. On account of his finiteness he does not realise his

[1] *Gitanjali*, 56. [2] *Sādhanā*, p. 41.
[3] *Fruit-Gathering*, LXXVIII.

aim. The content of his ideal passes beyond his existence. It has a reach beyond his grasp. He strives towards it, but it eludes his effort. He sees it as a vision beheld in dreaming, something ardently longed for.[1] The finite universe of persons and things represents to us the passage from the imperfect to the perfect. We see the road, the end is not yet. Through the world, the opportunities it affords, "they are coming, the pilgrims, one and all—coming to their true inheritance of the world."[2] The world is but the progress of pilgrims in their quest for the infinite. Every object in it cries out, "I want thee, only thee," and struggles to attain immortal life.

V

Man cannot reach the ideal so long as fragments of finiteness stick to him, so long as his intellect, emotion, and will are bound in the realm of finite nature. The finite intellect reduces the universe to the opposites of self and not-self, organism and environment, and leaves us there without revealing to us the final unity in which these relative opposites

[1] See *Gitanjali*, 13. [2] *Sādhāna*, p. 34.

rest. The ultimate unity breaks itself into the two factors of subject and object, man and nature. Intellect reads the manifestations, but misses the unity in which the two are gathered together. It exults in the strife of the opposites which is the play of the universe. The whole in which these distinctions are, not abolished, but overcome, the unity which is the final or the ultimate explanation of the things, is not grasped by it. What it does is to break up the world-poem and discover in it "the law of its rhythms, the measurement of its expansion and contraction, movement and use, the pursuit of its evolution of forms and character." These are no doubt "true achievements of the mind," but Rabindranath says, "We cannot stop there." Our thought cannot finally rest in them. We are in the hands of opposites still. The Upanishad says: "You will have fear so long as there is dualism." The universe of intellect "is like a railway station; but the station platform is not our home."[1] The world of intellect, with its distinctions of good and evil, truth and error, self and not-self, beauty and ugliness, is only a stage on the pathway to

[1] *Sādhanā*, p. 99.

reality. The intellectual vision is full of hard-and-fast lines of distinction. It makes the opposites absolute, and the system becomes full of contradictions; but if we pierce behind it we shall find that the rigid distinctions of intellect are fluid, and mingle in a wondrous whole. "This screen that thou hast raised is painted with innumerable figures with the brush of the night and the day. Behind it thy seat is woven in wondrous mysteries of curves, casting away all barren lines of straightness."[1] Beyond the two, beyond the finite and the infinite, we have the Absolute, which the finite intellect cannot grasp. Our mind cannot reach it. Our soul looks into the dim unknown to catch sight of it, but cannot find it where we come across motor cars and aeroplanes. Our vision is external, and God is not there; our vision is turned inside, and God is not there.

> If I say that He is within me, the universe is ashamed:
> If I say that He is without me, it is falsehood.[2]

We shall not see Him until we see Him everywhere, in and out, in darkness and in light. In the drama of Job it is put in the mouth

[1] *Gitanjali*, 71. [2] *Kabir's Poems*, IX.

of Zophar: "Canst thou by searching find out God? canst thou find out the Almighty unto perfection? It is high as heaven; what canst thou do? deeper than Sheol; what canst thou know?" The intuitive insight by which we can see God, the intellect cannot give. The Absolute is the highest unity from which all being proceeds; but it is so exalted and so exquisite that none of our conceptions can adequately describe it. Its overflowing life breaks through all intellectual barriers. A simple childlike vision, purified and purged of all prejudices, can get at it. When the soul is absorbed in God, it sees Him. "The soul that knows Brahman becomes Brahman." Reasoning and argument are of no avail. Syllogism does not give us its spirit. It is deeper than demonstration. Intelligence cannot fathom the depths of that divine mystery. He is a God who hideth Himself. He can be "felt in the dark, but not seen in the day."[1] He can only be known intuitively. Rabindranath says: "The vision of the Supreme One in our own soul is a direct and immediate intuition, not based on any ratiocination or demonstration at all."[2]

[1] *Stray Birds*, 87, p. 22.

[2] *Sādhanā*, p. 36.

To the eye of the finite intellect, it is darkness, impenetrable darkness. God is the King of the Dark Chamber. We are in a dark prison, surrounded by walls which our finiteness has raised, which separate us from others. Outside it there is light and no darkness. If suddenly the great vision appears to our untrained eyes, which can see objects only in the pleasure garden, if it reveals itself unexpectedly to our ordinary consciousness, sticking to the small strutting ego as if it were everything of consequence in the world, the vision will alarm the eyes and shake that consciousness to its foundations. Even to the high-souled Arjuna, with his soul full of divine fire and heart full of devotion to God, the tremendous vision of the Universal Form of God was insupportable, too terrific and awful for him to look upon. By its exceeding brilliance it will dazzle the eyes of mortal man. God who shows himself in a moment of great suffering will look terrible.

Black, black—oh, thou art black like the everlasting night! I only looked on thee for one dreadful instant. The blaze of the fire fell on your features—you looked like the awful night when a comet swings fearfully into our ken

—oh, then I closed my eyes—I could not look on you any more. Black as the threatening storm-cloud, black as the shoreless sea with the spectral red tint of twilight on its tumultuous waves![1]

For one awful moment the Princess saw into the heart of things with the eyes of eternity, and had visions of suns grown cold, universes frozen. We cannot see either in perfect darkness or in perfect light. Both are dark to us—one with the excess of brightness, the other with the lack of it. We want a mixture of opposites everywhere, and that we have in our solid-seeming world. The Princess in the drama of *The King of the Dark Chamber*, which describes the eternal quest of the soul for its kindred, wishes to see her husband and dear lord in the empirical world, where we have summer houses and motor cars, in the world of time, space, and causation. She wants to see him as an object among objects. She cannot reach him thus. The scientist says: You can sweep the wide heavens with the telescope but will not find God. Even so the Princess, when her vision is confined to the empirical world, may grow sceptic about

[1] *Dark Chamber*, p. 110. "God's right hand is gentle, but terrible is his left hand" (*Stray Birds*, No. 211).

the existence of God. "It strikes me, Kaundilya, that these people haven't got a King at all. They have somehow managed to keep the rumour afloat."[1] The existence of God is put down for a fiction or a hypothesis, contrived by the cunning, perhaps to keep the wretch in good order. Life becomes a despairing question and God a problem. He is near to her if she looks from the proper angle of vision, but He is far off if she adopts the empirical standpoint. The Absolute is a phantom that eludes her grasp. So long as the Princess wants to find God, who is ever in love with her, where she sees trees and animals, birds and stones, she cannot find Him.

The reason is that the Supreme is not an object which we can see with our finite eyes. It is the very light by which we see all objects. How can we see it as an object when it is both the subject and the object, when it is the light by which we see and the light which we see? There is nothing else than light to see it by. If we turn ourselves rightly, we shall see it everywhere. Ourself and the whole universe are eternal witnesses to its presence. It is the

[1] *Dark Chamber*, p. 18.

life of life, the self of self. It is in our very heart. We need not fathom the sea, or sweep the sky; we need not ascend into heaven or descend into the deep to reach it. A conversion of soul is what is needed. If we break through the ordinary gaze we shall find it. Our cherished illusions must go. The vulgar wisdom of the masses should be recognised to be vulgar. An inversion of the secular into the religious consciousness is needed. If we get rid of the finiteness, and rise above the intellectual level and pierce behind the veil, we shall see it face to face. To see God we should transfer ourselves to another dimension of reality. We should break down the barrier of individuality and relax the despotism of the senses; our ignorance will then be removed. We escape from the light of separation and see God as the transcendent darkness in which the whole universe is bathed. Surangama says: "A day came when all the rebel in me knew itself beaten, and then my whole nature bowed down in humble resignation on the dust of the earth. And then I saw . . . I saw that he was as matchless in beauty as in terror. Oh, I was saved, I was rescued."[1] We shall then see our ordinary consciousness to be the real darkness and the transcendent one to be the perfect radiance of Eternity. The Princess says: "Your sight repelled me because I had sought to find you in the pleasure garden, in my Queen's chambers: there even your meanest servant looks handsomer than you. That fever of longing has left my eyes for ever. You are not beautiful, my lord—you stand beyond all comparisons!" While the supreme is bright and clear to the religious intuition, it is misty and dark to the cold intellect. It is "dark from its surpassing brightness . . . as the shining of the sun on his course is as darkness to weak eyes."[2] Vaughan in his "The Night" says:

> There is in God, some say,
> A deep but dazzling darkness, as men here
> Say, it is late and dusky because they
> See not all clear.
> O for that night! where I in Him
> Might live invisible and dim.

To the finite consciousness God is far away; to the religious soul He is quite near. God is present, yet absent. The Bhagavad-

[1] *Dark Chamber*, p. 43.

[2] Tauler.

gita says: "Near and far away is That." The Isa Upanishad says: "He is far and also near." "When you think that He is not here, then you wander farther and farther away, and seek Him in vain with tears. Where He is far off, there He is unattainable: Where He is near, He is very bliss." "They have sung of Him as infinite and unattainable: but I in my meditations have seen Him without sight."[1] Tukaram, the Indian saint, says: "O man, why do you travel from place to place to search God? As the deer does not know that it possesses an invaluable thing called *kasthuri* (musk), so you do not know what is within you. Search God within you and you will find Him." Rabindranath says: "You were in the centre of my heart, therefore when my heart wandered she never found you."[2]

> The traveller has to knock at every alien door to come to his own, and one has to wander through all the outer worlds to reach the innermost shrine at the end.
>
> My eyes strayed far and wide before I shut them and said "Here art thou!"[3]

In thus transcending intellect by intuition

[1] *Kabir's Poems*, XVII.; see also XXI. and XXIII.
[2] *Fruit-Gathering*, LXIX.
[3] *Gitanjali*, 12.

we become childlike in our simplicity and innocence of the world's ways. Our knowledge is transformed into wisdom. "God waits for man to regain his childhood in wisdom."[1]

The eyes of the body are closed as in sleep for the eyes of spirit to open as in dreams. "Yea, when it sleeps, the mind is bright with eyes."[2] Thus Rabindranath, in common with other mystics, discriminates between the path of intuition, which is the way of wisdom born of love, and the path of intellect, which is the way of knowledge born of observation.[3] Intuition enables us to penetrate beneath outward appearances studied by science and see the life in things. It is a matter of experience or insight, which is coercive and certain. The design-argument, which makes God a matter of inference and not observation, is urged by Janardhan in *The King of the Dark Chamber*. "But look at the nice order and regularity prevailing all over the place—how do you explain it without a King?" This argument is put down for

[1] *Stray Birds*. [2] Aeschylus.
[3] See *Fruit-Gathering*, XX.

mere quibbling, as the question is to be decided by intuition. "Have you, or have you not, seen the King? Yes or no?"[1] Kabir sings: "They are blind who hope to see it by the light of reason, that reason which is the cause of separation. The house of Reason is very far away."[2] Reason, which can help us to weigh the dust or measure the air, cannot show us the face of God. The truly religious soul does not argue and infer, but meditates and waits for light. The poet, the artist, and the lover pursue this path of intuition; the mystic knows it, and lives in the full light of the vision.

VI

In the characterisations of God in the Vedanta writings and Rabindranath's works we find an identity of thought. The popular idea that the Brahman of the Vedanta is an abstract beyond is incorrect. Rabindranath protests against such a misconception. He says: "The infinite in India was not a thin nonentity, void of all content. The Rishis of

[1] *Dark Chamber*, p. 20. [2] *Kabir's Poems*, XCVII.

India asserted emphatically, 'To know Him in this life is to be true; not to know Him in this life is the desolation of death.' How to know Him then? 'By realising Him in each and all.' Not only in nature, but in the family, in society, and in the state, the more we realise the world-conscious in all, the better for us. Failing to realise it we turn our faces to destruction."[1] The Vedanta thinkers do not place God in the solitude of a world beyond. The hymn or *mantra* chanted every evening at the Bolpur school, "The God who is in fire, who is in water, who interpenetrates the whole world, who is in herbs, who is in trees, to that God I bow again and again," is from the Upanishads.[2] The Vedantic Absolute as much as Rabindranath's God is a concrete spirit.

> He is there where the tiller is tilling the hard ground and where the pathmaker is breaking stones.[3]

The mystics of all faiths and creeds, from the Rishis of Upanishads downwards, are at one in this belief in the immanence of God. St. Paul says: "He is above all, through all, and

[1] *Sādhanā*, p. 20; see *Personality*, pp. 56-57.
[2] Swetaswatara Upanishad, II-17.
[3] *Gitanjali*, 11.

in all." So too we read: "Raise the stone, and there thou shalt find me; cleave the wood, and there am I." It is meaningless to argue that the Vedantic Absolute is a barren nothing and Rabindranath's God a concrete something, and therefore Rabindranath is no Vedantin. The logic is irresistible; only the premisses are false.

Critics may urge that the Vedanta philosophy is ambiguous about the nature of God. True it says, God is All, but it also says God is nothing. "It is not this, not this." This dilemma of mysticism which makes God sometimes the All, sometimes nothing, is not peculiar to the Vedanta writings, but runs through all mystic literature. Rabindranath's poems are full of it. In some pages the Absolute is an abstract, formless, featureless unity, not a God who deserves to be adóred and worshipped. It is "the inscrutable without name and form."[1]

> But there, where spreads the infinite sky for the soul to take her flight in, reigns the stainless white radiance. There is no day nor night, nor form nor colour, and never, never a word.[2]

---

[1] *Gitanjali*, 95. [2] *Ibid.* 67.

On the other hand, in the same poem Rabindranath makes the whole universe the manifestation of God:

> Thou art the sky, and thou art the nest as well.[1]

Much the same thing is true of Kabir's utterances.

> He is neither manifest nor hidden, He is neither revealed nor unrevealed:
> There are no words to tell that which He is.[2]
> He is without form, without quality, without decay.[3]
> Only he knows it who has reached that region: it is other than all that is heard and said.
> No form, no body, no length, no breadth is seen there: how can I tell you that which it is.[4]

To represent the other current of his thought we may cite the following passage:

> He Himself is the tree, the seed, and the germ.
> He Himself is the flower, the fruit, and the shade.
> He Himself is the sun, the light, and the lighted.
> He Himself is Brahma, creature, and Maya.
> He Himself is the manifold form, the infinite space;
> He is the breath, the word, and the meaning.
> He Himself is the limit and the limitless: and beyond both the limited and the limitless is He, the Pure Being.
> He is the Immanent Mind in Brahma and in the creature.[5]

---

[1] *Gitanjali*, 67.
[2] *Kabir's Poems*, IX.
[3] *Ibid.* XXVI.
[4] *Ibid.* LXXVI.
[5] *Ibid.* VII.

The Upanishads are full of such apparently contradictory descriptions, for they are only the records of the spiritual experiences of the sages of India. "He is not this, He is not that."[1] "It is neither coarse nor fine, neither sharp nor long, neither red like fire nor fluid like water; it is without shadow, without darkness, without air, without water, without attachment, without taste, without smell, without eyes, without ears, without speech, without mind, without light, without breath, without mouth, without measure, having no within and no without; it devours nothing and no one devours it."[2] To represent the other tendency we have the Chandogya, which says: "All this universe has the Supreme deity for its life. That deity is truth. He is the Universal soul. Thou art He, Swethakethu."[3] The Mundaka Upanishad says: "This immortal Brahma, to the right and the left, below and above, all pervading, Brahma is this All, this infinite world."[4] The contradiction between the two accounts is only apparent and not real. If by means of our finite intellect we

[1] Brihadaranyaka Upanishad, ii. 3. 6.

[2] *Ibid.* iii. 8; see also iv. 4. 22.

[3] *Ibid.* vi. 7.

[4] *Ibid.* ii. 11; see also Swethaswathara, iv. 2-4.

try to reach the Absolute we shall fail in our attempts. The Kena Upanishad says: "It is far from the known and above the unknown." The Taittiriya says: "Words together with the mind return without comprehending it." The Absolute unity is opposed to the intellectual duality, and the intellectual account of the Absolute remains a negative one. But when we rise above the plane of intellect to religion, poetry, and philosophy we see it face to face. When we say that the Absolute is above the grasp of intellect, we do not mean that it is opposed to it. Only in the Absolute the intellectual is realised. "In love all the contradictions of existence merge themselves and are lost. Only in love are unity and duality not at variance."[1] At the intuitional level the Absolute is the all-comprehending love with whom we can commune, whom we can love, adore, and worship. The Absolute is the whole Universe. The creation is the dance, *leela*, or the play of the Absolute. "The Creator brought into being the game of joy. The Earth is his Joy. . . . In play is the creation spread out. In play it is established."[2]

[1] *Sādhanā*, 114.

[2] *Kabir's Poems*, LXXXII.

Rabindranath's God as much as the Vedantic Absolute is a concrete Universal.

VII

Now the question arises, Is Rabindranath's God a person and not the impersonal Absolute of the Vedanta? Yes: *Gitanjali* makes of God a person. The Vedanta Philosophy in all its stages of development provides for such a conception. Art, philosophy, and religion are the specialised modes in which the Absolute presents itself to mankind. God is a trinity because man is. The human individual is a unity of intellect, emotion, and will, and the Supreme Ideal, to satisfy sentiment, will, and reason, appears as Supreme Beauty, Supreme Good, Supreme Truth. And as the human individual is a unity of the three, and as these elements cannot conflict with each other, and as no one of them can complete its idea except as it gathers into itself the two others, even so there is no discord between the different aspects of truth, beauty, and goodness in the Supreme Ideal. This ideal shows itself to man's capacity for joy as Supreme Beauty, to his capacity for knowledge as Supreme

Truth, to his capacity to act, as Supreme Good. The contents of the three do not vary, though their form does. Art, philosophy, and religion are different forms and expressions of worship and different ways of approach to God. The particular method depends upon the temperamental characteristics with which the Creator has enriched human nature. All souls —saints, sages, and seers—seek union with God. Mystic souls of an emotional and imaginative cast of mind express their devotion by love, worship, and adoration. They make a person of the object of their love. In Rabindranath the art aspect predominates. His wealth of imagination, force of feeling, and intensity of passion turn his words into music and poetry. The poems of *Gitanjali* are the offerings of the finite to the infinite. The relation between the two is conceived of as that between the lover and the beloved—an analogy employed by the mystics the world over. Throughout oriental literature, this analogy is constantly used to express the true relationship between the human soul and God. Radha's passionate devotion to Krishna is the symbol of the soul's yearning for God. When Krishna, to draw all creation to him, sings the divine music of his flute, she listens to it and gives up her all for His sake. The analogy of human love holds, in that in perfect love we have two yet one, a single life led by a man and a woman.[1] The surrender of the soul, the fulfilment of love, and the union with the other spirit, characteristic of human love, are present in the longing for the Absolute. But if we press this analogy too far we get all sorts of difficulties. Ultimately there will be no divorce between head and heart, reason and faith.[2] Rabindranath is intellectual enough to recognise that the Vedantic Absolute which he believes to be the ultimate philosophical unity does not lend itself to intellectual description. But being an

[1] The Persian poet sings:

Four eyes met. There were changes in two souls.
And now I cannot remember whether he is a man and I a woman,
Or he a woman and I a man. All I know is,
There were two, love came, and there is one.

Rabindranath writes: "In love, at one of its poles you find the personal, at the other the impersonal. At one you have the positive assertion—Here I am; at the other the equally strong denial—I am not. Without this ego what is love? And again, with only this ego how can love be possible?" (*Sādhanā*, pp. 114-115).

[2] Cf. That Beauty, Good, and Knowledge, are three sisters
That doat upon each other, friends to man,
Living together under the same roof,
And never can be sunder'd without tears.
Tennyson, "Palace of Art."

artist, he translates his spiritual experience into material symbols. The language is metaphorical, and if literally interpreted would lead to absurdities and contradictions. Miss Evelyn Underhill remarks in her admirable introduction to *Kabir's Poems*: "It is a marked characteristic of mystical literature that the great contemplatives, in their effort to convey to us the nature of their communion with the supersensuous, are inevitably driven to employ some form of sensuous imagery: coarse and inaccurate as they know such imagery to be, even at the best." If from the poems of *Gitanjali* we infer that God is a person over against man, we make a mistake. To Rabindranath God is not a being seated high up in the heavens, but a spirit immanent in the whole Universe of persons and things. Rabindranath's love is a spiritual love above sex, unintelligible to the world at large, a love which loses itself in the sea of the Absolute to "melt and vanish away in the dark, or it may be in a smile of the white morning, in a coolness of purity transparent."[1] The Absolute of philosophy becomes the God of religion, to all

[1] *Gitanjali*, 80.

followers of the Bhakti school. Iswara, the highest manifestation of the Absolute, is the personal Lord of the Universe. The distinction of the lover and the loved is kept up till the last point, when in perfect love the two become one. The personal God is then dissolved in the Absolute. If Rabindranath is viewed as a worshipper of a personal God, he may be looked upon as the living example of the long and noble succession of religious devotees of whom India is justly proud, including among others Manikkavasagar, Ramanuja, Maddhwa, Ramananda, Vedanta Desikar, Jnaneswar, Namdev, Vallabha Charya, Kabir, Chandidas, Chaithanya, Nanak, Dadu, Tulasidas, and Tukaram. This Bhakti school has had a continuous history from the very beginnings of reflection in India. A Christian critic, Dr. Macnicol, says: "Theism is both ancient in the land and indigenous to the soil. . . . No one need suppose that the ideas that bhakti connotes are a foreign importation into India."[1] The

[1] *Indian Theism*, p. 275. Rabindranath says: "We discern two opposite currents in India's divine lore (*brahma vidya*)—the abstract God and the personal God, monism and duality. There cannot be worship unless we admit duality, and yet there cannot be devotion unless we fix our gaze on One" (*Modern Review*, August 1913). The two are aspects of the one Godhead.

critics who make Rabindranath a borrower from Christianity betray an astonishing lack of "historic conscience"—a charge generally urged against Indians. The Absolute of philosophy and the God of religion have both a place in the Vedanta system. Those who draw a hard-and-fast line of distinction between the two will never be able to understand the Vedanta philosophy. What Richard Garbe says of the Bhagavadgita is true of other Vedanta writings: "The doctrines which are here put into the mouth of Krishna present a remarkable combination of pantheistic and monotheistic ideas, of philosophical thoughts and of pure and deeply religious faith in God."[1] The formless Absolute has to be conceived as a being of form by the finite individual. To put it the other way, we can say that the Absolute, which is above the pairs of opposites of beauty and ugliness, truth and error, good and evil, still appears for the sake of man as perfect Beauty, perfect Truth, and perfect Goodness. "The Perfect decks itself in beauty for the love of the Imperfect."[2] The

[1] *Encyclopædia of Religion and Ethics*, vol. ii. p. 536.

[2] *Stray Birds*, No. 62.

following words, quoted in Maharshi Devendranath Tagore's *Autobiography*, admirably depict the contrition of the devotee for the confusion of spirit due to his finiteness:

> O spiritual guide of the Universe, Thou art without form:
> Yet that I have conceived Thine image in the act of meditation;
> That I have ignored Thine inexpressibility by words of praise;
> That I have set at naught Thy omnipresence by making pilgrimages, and in other ways,—
> For these three transgressions committed through confusion of spirit, O Almighty God, I implore Thy forgiveness.

CHAPTER II

THE PHILOSOPHY OF RABINDRANATH TAGORE—II

Life-breath is the breath of immortality. The body ends in ashes. O my will, remember thy deeds. O God, O Fire, thou knowest all deeds. Lead us through good paths to fulfilment. Separate from us the crooked sin. To thee we offer our speech of salutation.—*Isa Upanishad.*

Whoso takes the world's life on him and his own lays down,
He, dying so, lives. SWINBURNE.

I

THE acquisition of the true insight into things is the mark of religion. That insight we can have only when our souls have so expanded as to feel for the whole universe. This expansion of soul, this "widening of the range of feeling," can be achieved not by adding to our possessions, not by extending our dominions, but by giving up our finite self. "We have, however, to pay a price for this attainment of the freedom of consciousness. What is the price? It is to give oneself away. Our soul can realise itself truly only by denying itself. The Upanishad says, *Thou shalt gain by giving away, Thou shalt not covet.*"[1] "The consciousness of the infinite in us proves itself by our joy in giving ourselves out of our abundance. And then our work is the process of our renunciation, it is one with our life. It is like the flowing of the river, which is the river itself."[2] Spiritual attainment consists in giving away or renunciation. We have to conquer the world by caring naught for it. Self-denial is the path to self-realisation. This idea is brought out by the image of the lamp and the oil. "The lamp contains its oil, which it holds securely in its close grasp and guards from the least loss. Thus is it separate from all other objects around it and is miserly. But when lighted it finds its meaning at once; its relation with all things far and near is established, and it freely sacrifices its fund of oil to feed the flame."[3] With the annihilation of self comes the fulfilment of love. The self-centred life becomes God-centred. Man shall not see

[1] *Sādhanā*, p. 19. [2] *Personality*, p. 63. [3] *Sādhanā*, p. 76.

God and live, goes the saying. Certainly not. So long as he is man he cannot see Him. When he sees Him he ceases to be man.[1] Before that vastness and splendour man's individuality shrinks and crumbles into dust. The all-dwelling love invades, submerges, and overwhelms the individual consciousness. The whole individual — body, mind, and soul—is given up to God.

> From the blue sky an eye shall gaze upon me and summon me in silence. Nothing will be left for me, nothing whatever, and utter death shall I receive at thy feet.[2]

This state of supreme bliss is not "death but completeness." It is the perfection of consciousness, where there is no dust or darkness to obscure the vision. It is an utter clearness and transparency through which God's rays pass and repass without let or hindrance. It is complete harmony, perfect love, and supreme joy. In that all-embracing consciousness the finite and the infinite are enfolded in one. "The inward and the out-

[1] "Fully to realise the existence of the Absolute is for finite beings impossible. In order thus to know we should have to be, and then we should not exist" (Bradley: *Appearance and Reality*).

[2] *Gitanjali*, 98.

ward are become as one sky, the Infinite and the finite are united."[1] It is self-transcendence, not annihilation. It is life eternal. "It is the extinction of the lamp in the morning light; not the abolition of the sun."[2] A passage in Nettleship hits the point well. "Suppose that all human beings felt habitually to each other as they now do occasionally to those they love best. All the pain of the world will be swallowed up in doing good. So far as we can conceive of such a state it will be one in which there will be no individuals at all, but an universal being, in and for another; where being took the form of consciousness, it would be consciousness of another which was also oneself—a common consciousness. Such would be the atonement of the world." Mr. Bosanquet asks us to think of the attitude demanded of one by a masterpiece of art. "You scarcely recognise yourself, when for a moment Shakespeare or Beethoven has laid his spell on you."[3] In human life we soon slip back from this condition of self-forgetfulness; in the supreme state of bliss we have a perpetuation

[1] *Kabir's Poems*, XVII. ; see also *Sādhanā*, p. 43.

[2] *Sādhanā*, p. 82 ; see Brihadaranyaka Upanishad, iv. 3. 21.

[3] *Gifford Lectures*, vol. i. p. 260.

of this condition. The final state is a total transformation of the personality into an explicit organ of the Absolute. The independent false will is destroyed, the perfect surrender of the will to God makes the will the Divine will. We obtain this condition, not by abstraction, but by comprehension, not by exclusion, but by inclusion. It is therefore fulness of life. "Life dies into the fulness."[1] The individual tries to realise the infinite within him, adore it, clasp it with affection, and ultimately become one with it. Till this goal is reached, man is caught in the world process. When it is reached the false individuality separating man from God becomes extinct. "When one knows thee, then alien there is none, then no door is shut."[2] The soul is then prepared to meet death or anything even more fearful than that. For it then shares the life eternal which death cannot defeat. "My whole body and my limbs have thrilled with his touch who is beyond touch; and if the end comes here, let it come."[3] The white radiance of eternity fills him, and puts fire into his heart

[1] *Fruit-Gathering*, LIV.

[2] *Gitanjali*, 63; see also Brihadaranyaka Upanishad, ii. 4. 14.

[3] *Gitanjali*, 96.

and music into his soul. He becomes endowed with eternal youth and strength, and fills the world with light.[1]

II

Side by side with this view of eternal life, we also come across the doctrine of reincarnation.

> The child cries out when from the right breast the mother takes it away, in the very next moment to find in the left one its consolation.[2]
>
> Death belongs to life as birth does.
>
> The walk is in the raising of the foot as in the laying of it down.[3]

With the Hindu philosophers, Rabindranath believes in the gradual perfection of individuals till the ideal is attained. The soul has to pass through many lives before the goal can be reached. "Thou hast made me endless, such is thy pleasure. This frail vessel thou emptiest again and again, and fillest it ever with fresh life. The time that my journey takes is long and the way of it long. I came out on the chariot of the first gleam of light, and pursued my voyage through the wildernesses of worlds leaving my

[1] See *Sādhanā*, p. 14; Bhagavadgita, ii. 55-58.

[2] *Gitanjali*, 95.

[3] *Stray Birds*, 268.

track on many a star and planet."[1] In the progress towards perfection, man, owing to the weakness of his flesh, has to renew his body, and this renewal is what we call death. "It is thou who drawest the veil of night upon the tired eyes of the day to renew its sight in a fresher gladness of awakening."[2] Death is only a preparation for a higher and fuller life.

In the matter of future life, Rabindranath is at one with the Rishis of the Upanishads, who also hold the two views of immortality and reincarnation, the life of completeness and perfection and the life which continues endlessly. Both these views are valid in their respective spheres. So long as man is finite and does not give up his selfish nature, his destiny is not fulfilled, and the final consummation of becoming one with God is not attained, he is in the moral life struggling hard to attain the end which he does not get. He perpetually approximates to the goal, but never reaches it. For a finite being to achieve this impossible task, as Kant urges, infinite time is not enough. So long as man identifies himself with his finite, fleeting personality, he is

[1] *Gitanjali*, 1 and 12. [2] *Ibid.* 25.

subject to the law of infinite progress and perpetual approximation. As Indians have it, he is bound in the cycle of births and deaths. He goes from life to life; death becomes only an incident in life, a change from one scene to another. But when the individual completely surrenders himself to the universal life, and the self becomes one with the supreme, then he gains the bliss of heaven and shares the life eternal. He is lifted above the travail of births and deaths, and above mere succession in time, to which alone death is relevant. In the moral life, where we have the individual attempting to reach the goal, we have the endless succession in time which belongs to the finite; but when moral life is swallowed up in religion, then the spirit transcends time and attains a timeless immortality.

III

The Absolute is the organic whole consisting of the different elements of matter, life, consciousness, and intellect.[1] These are the expressions of the whole; but if they set themselves up for the whole, we are in the

[1] See the Taittiriya Upanishad.

region of *maya.* As parts of the Absolute they are real; as unconnected with it they are illusory. *Avidya* or ignorance of the real nature of the world and man's place in it chains us in the bonds of *maya.* Then the finite existence becomes a *pathos,* and nature a bondage from which we should escape. In the world of *maya* our individuality appears to be ultimate; but if we overcome this illusion, we find our individual consciousness to be a unique expression of the universal. "Everything has this dualism of *maya* and *satyam,* appearance and truth. . . . Our self is *maya* where it is merely individual and finite, where it considers its separateness as absolute; it is *satyam* where it recognises its essence in the universal and infinite, in the supreme self, in Paramătman."[1] In the Devi Bhagavata it is said that when Shakti turns towards the world she is *maya*; when she turns towards the Lord she is seen to be himself.[2] It is wrong to think that the world has an independent existence. "This world-song is never for a moment separated from its singer. Music and the musician are in-

[1] *Sādhanā,* p. 85.

[2] See *Fruit-Gathering,* V.

separable."[1] The play of the universe is centred round God.

> The piper pipes in the centre, hidden from sight,
> And we become frantic, we dance.[2]

If we separate the two, we break up the real into the two abstracts of the finite and the infinite, which are both unreal and illusory. The mere finite is like "a lamp without its light," a "violin without its music." The mere infinite is "utter emptiness." The two are real in their union. "The infinite and the finite are one, as song and singing are one."[3] It is only in marriage with the finite that the infinite can bear fruit; divorced from it, it remains barren. The unity of God is realised only through the many. "The real with its meaning read wrong and emphasis misplaced is the unreal."[4] *Maya*, thus, is a phantom that is and is not.

IV

When we perceive the real significance of nature and society we find they are there for the purpose of enabling us to reach the infinite. The ideal is to be attained, not by escaping

[1] *Sādhanā*, p. 143.
[2] *The Cycle of Spring.*
[3] *Personality*, pp. 56-57.
[4] *Stray Birds*, 254.

from the confusions of the world of sense, but by spiritualising them. Rabindranath does not look upon the body as the tomb or the prison of the soul from which it has to be liberated. For him man is bound up with nature; the human spirit is wedded to the material organism. Contact with the body, instead of being a tainting of the purity of the soul, is just the condition necessary for developing its nature. Nature is not, as such, evil. It all depends. If the individual rests in his sensuous nature self-satisfied, without directing his vision to God, then nature turns out to be a tempter. If, on the other hand, it is made to become the organ of the higher spirit, nothing can be said against it. By itself nature is a-moral. The spirit quickens it. It is the duty of man to transfigure the natural, break its externalism and transitoriness, and make it fully express the spirit for which it is intended.[1]

If we think nature to be separate from God,

[1] Tennyson, who comes nearest to this idea, overlooks the essentially positive relation of body to mind. He seems to think that matter is incompatible with spirit:

> "This weight of body and limb
> Are they not sign and symbol of thy division from Him?"

we are in the world of *maya*. But if God is immanent in the universe, how can we refuse as dross the material body? The creative love of God is the source of the universe which is destined to reflect in itself the fulness of Divine perfection. The world is not the denial of God. It is His living image and not His enemy. It has to be fashioned into the symbol and instrument of the spirit. The body should be made the sign and utterance of the soul. "The flowers grow out of the dirt, but the foulness of the source is abolished in the flower itself."[1] Rabindranath protests against ignoring the senses.

> No, I will never shut the doors of my senses. The delights of sight and hearing and touch will bear thy delight.[2]

Rabindranath says:

> The dust receives insult and in return offers her flowers.[3]

The world of nature is neither a delusion of the Creator nor a snare of the devil. It is the playground where we have to build our souls.

Similarly the world of persons and things

[1] Tucker. [2] *Gitanjali*, 73. [3] *Stray Birds*, 101, p. 26.

is not something to be escaped from. It is there to enable the finite individual to reach his goal. "The entire world is given to us, and all our powers have their final meaning in the faith that by their help we are to take possession of our patrimony."[1] Nature and society are but the instruments by which to elicit the infiniteness of the finite being, the material to help the finite to work out its destiny. The whole universe is penetrated and vitalised by the living spirit, and so responds to the call of spirit. Not a fragment of it which is not deeply interesting and divine, if we approach it in the right way. Anything can be made the channel of approach to God, an entrance to immortality. "All paths lead to thee." Nothing in the visible world is too low for the use of spirit. The dull dense world has openings throughout to the white radiance.

> God the great giver can open the whole universe to our gaze, in the narrow space of a single lane.[2]
>
> Infinite is thy mansion, my lord.[3]

Earth is crammed with heaven; all exist-

[1] *Sādhanā*, p. 137. [2] *Reminiscences*, p. 221.
[3] *Gitanjali*, 87.

ence is suffused with God. "Why, the whole country is all filled and crammed and packed with the King."[1] As a Greek thinker has it, the earth is bound by a chain of gold to heaven. The smallest details of the world contain prophecies of the unknown. The universe is everywhere a gate through which we can enter our spiritual heritage. Strike it anywhere, lay hold of it anywhere, it opens to the mansion of God. "He comes, comes, ever comes. Every moment and every age, every day and every night, he comes, comes, ever comes."[2] It is never too late to become a recruit to God's army. "At the end of the day I hasten in fear lest thy gate be shut; but I find that yet there is time."[3] If we miss an opportunity, it is dead and gone, never more to recur. It is no good repenting after the event. At any moment the night may come when no man shall work. We must seize the opportunities as the world presents them, for they do not come at our invitation. We must be ever ready to receive God, for it may well happen that when He comes we

[1] *Dark Chamber*, p. 14.
[2] *Gitanjali*, 45.
[3] *Ibid.* 82.

are not ready, and when we are ready He does not come.[1]

The things of nature and the events of the world will cause trouble and vexation of spirit, if, instead of utilising them for spiritual and unselfish ends, we make use of them for our own sensation and enjoyment.

> Why did the lamp go out?
>
> I shaded it with my cloak to save it from the wind, that is why the lamp went out.
>
> Why did the flower fade?
>
> I pressed it to my heart with anxious love, that is why the flower faded.
>
> Why did the stream dry up?
>
> I put a dam across it to have it for my use, that is why the stream dried up.
>
> Why did the harp-string break?
>
> I tried to force a note that was beyond its power, that is why the harp-string is broken.[2]

"Man's abiding happiness is not in getting anything but in giving himself up to what is greater than himself, to ideas which are larger than his individual self, the idea of his country, of humanity, of God."[3] The world gives us opportunities for surrendering our

[1] See *The Gardener*, 8, 36, 57, and 66.

[2] *The Gardener*, 52.

[3] *Sādhanā*, p. 152.

all. There is a touch of the eternal in all such surrenders to unselfish ideals, or dedications to high causes. We then feel the feet of God and forget ourselves. A high and noble ideal releases the self. It delivers us from our selfishness and opens the gateway to immortality. Even the common things of earth's everyday experience, if we wholeheartedly give up ourselves to them, would take us to heaven. In such transactions the characteristic features of religion are present. "Whenever we find a devotion which makes the finite self seem as nothing and some reality to which it attaches itself seem as all, we have the essentially religious attitude."[1] The transcendent value of the ideal and the utter prostration of the self are complementary aspects of one experience. We should say in the presence of the ideal: "You are all my world. I am lost in you."[2] Look at Arjuna's address to Chitra. "You alone are perfect; you are the wealth of the world, the end of all poverty, the goal of all efforts, the one woman! Others there are who can be

[1] Bosanquet, *Gifford Lectures*, vol. ii. p. 235.

[2] *The Gardener*, 46 and 48.

but slowly known. While to see you for a moment is to see perfect completeness once and for ever."[1] Chitra responds to this appeal: "I heard his call, 'Beloved, my most beloved.' And all my forgotten lives united as one and responded to it. I said, 'Take me, take all I am.' And I stretched out my arms to him. . . . Heaven and earth, time and space, pleasure and pain, death and life merged together in an unbearable ecstasy."[2] There is nothing more heavenly on earth than the surrender of the soul of a woman to the man she loves. Self-transcendence, the mark of all spiritual experience, is present in the devoted passion for the pursuit of science, art, and morality. In human love we have such moments. "Only for a few fragrant hours we two have been made immortal."[3] We then touch the hem of the garment of God, though we do not know it. "Entering my heart unbidden even as one of the common crowd, unknown to me, my king, thou didst press the signet of eternity upon many a fleeting moment of my life."[4] Religious

[1] *Chitra*, pp. 18 and 19.
[2] *Ibid.* p. 24.
[3] *The Gardener*, 44.
[4] *Gitanjali*, 43.

experience is nothing more than this utter neglect of the self and surrender to God who captures our body, mind, and soul. It is a breaking up of our selfishness and a reaching out towards the whole. The finite ideals we sometimes disinterestedly pursue will sooner or later manifest their inadequacy to satisfy the needs of the soul. Though perfect human love approximates to this, we soon recognise that it cannot satisfy the infinite craving in us for heavenly perfection. It may open the way to it, but it can never be the end. "If their love has its absolute centre in creatures, whether brute or human, then there will be misery, and they will suffer from disappointments through sickness, death, and separation; but if they have the consciousness of the infinite personality in the centre and background of their personal life, then the power of love will be fully satisfied, and all the gaps will be filled, and their joys and sorrows will join their hands in a harmony of fulfilment which is blessedness."[1] We long to become one with the perfect ideal. "In

[1] Tagore's parting message to the women of America, *Current Opinion*, April 1917.

that devastation, in the utter nakedness of spirit, let us become one in beauty." No finite object can satisfy this craving. "Alas for my vain desire! Where is this hope for union except in thee, my God?"[1] Finite ideals will have to be transmuted into the infinite before the soul can get perfect satisfaction through them.

V

It follows that the God-possessed soul will spend itself in the service of man. Just as to the lover there is nothing unclean or impure in the loved one's body, even so to the lover of God there is nothing untouchable in the great body of God, the world of men. Withdrawal from social work may be the temptation of the abstract mystic who turns away in disgust from the world of discord and contradiction, but to him the infinite will remain an abstract barren negative. It does not greatly matter whether we call it being or non-being. It is a question of taste or temperament. But, as Kabir says, we "find naught

[1] *The Gardener*, 50.

in that emptiness."[1] But loyalty to God the highest universal is meaningless if it does not embody itself in work for man the finite particular. The one is not beyond the many but is in the many. To the true mystic who realises by direct experience the central harmony of the universe there is "no mystery beyond the present; no striving for the impossible; no shadow behind the charm; no groping in the depth of the dark."[2] The infinite is not other than the finite, but is the finite transfigured.[3] Life eternal is not the life beyond time, but is the life of recognition, here and now, of all things in the self, and the self in all things. The religious soul dwells in the world and helps to make it more fit for the habitation of God. As it is said, "Inasmuch as ye have done it unto one of the least of these my brethren, ye have done it unto me." Those who consider that the worship of God will help us to reach the goal, even though we are indifferent and hostile to the service and welfare of man, do not know the secret of salvation. God is not in the king's temple, even though "twenty millions of gold went to

[1] *Poems*, XX. [2] *The Gardener*, 16. [3] See *Gitanjali*, 78.

the making of that marvel of art, and it was consecrated to God with costly rites"; for the temple was built in the year when thousands of people whose houses have been burned stood vainly asking for help at his door.[1]

The idea of divine immanence requires, first of all, individual purity—purity of body, mind, heart, and will. The methods of *yoga*, *jnana*, *bhakti*, and *karma* are to be adopted for the development and discipline of the soul.[2]

> Life of my life, I shall ever try to keep my body pure, knowing that thy living touch is upon all my limbs.
>
> I shall ever try to keep all untruths out from my thoughts, knowing that thou art that truth which has kindled the light of reason in my mind.
>
> I shall ever try to drive all evils away from my heart and keep my love in flower, knowing that thou hast thy seat in the inmost shrine of my heart.
>
> And it shall be my endeavour to reveal thee in my actions, knowing it is thy power gives me strength to act.[3]

The consciousness of Divine immanence demands social justice. Every man should be looked upon as an end in himself and not as a means. On this familiar text of the Upanishads, the Bible, the Bhagavadgita, and Kant, Rabindranath comments, with special reference to the

[1] *Fruit-Gathering*, XXIV.

[2] See the Bhagavadgita, xvii. 14-16.

[3] *Gitanjali*, 4.

modern problems of slum life, sweating, prostitution, and political exploitation. "In the lands where cannibalism is prevalent man looks upon man as his food. In such a country civilisation can never thrive, for there man loses his higher value and is made common indeed. . . . Our desires blind us to the *truth* that there is in man, and this is the greatest wrong done by ourselves to our own soul. It deadens our consciousness, and is but a gradual method of spiritual suicide. It produces ugly sores in the body of civilisation, gives rise to its hovels and brothels, its vindictive penal codes, its cruel prison systems, its organised methods of exploiting foreign races to the extent of permanently injuring them by depriving them of the discipline of self-government and means of self-defence."[1] Here we have an eloquent expression of Rabindranath's deep hatred of tyranny and social injustice and thirst for social betterment. The true mission or destiny of the religious soul is not isolation or renunciation. It is to be a member of society recognising the infinite and boundless possibilities of man, and offering oneself up entirely

[1] *Sādhanā*, pp. 108 and 109.

and exhaustlessly to the service of one's fellows. The Bhagavadgita says: "Whoso enjoys without offering to the Gods their gifts, he is verily a thief."[1] The mystic's feeling of kinship or solidarity with the universe expresses itself in the work for a changed earth and a happier humanity. Sustained by the vision of man made perfect, his love goes out to every creature, the hungry and the thirsty, the sick and the imbecile, the stranger and the naked; for does not God live in them all? Is not a child born in the slum God's creation? "Here is thy footstool and there rest thy feet where live the poorest, and lowliest, and lost."[2]

VI

The liberated soul of the true saint does not wish to escape from this world but tries to improve it. But all his work will be rooted in an inner peace and repose. It is the same kind of activity as that which characterises the divine. It is true that it is bliss or delight. "From joy are born all creatures, by joy they are sustained, towards joy they progress, and into joy they enter." But this joy expresses

[1] iii. 12. [2] *Gitanjali*, 10.

itself in laws, which seemed to be bonds fettering it, while really the laws are the expression of love or freedom. "Fire burns for fear of him; the Sun shines by fear of him, and for fear of him the winds the clouds and death perform their office."[1] Law and Love are one in the Absolute. Even so in the liberated soul perfect service is perfect freedom. How can he whose joy is in Brahma live in inaction? "Our master himself has joyfully taken upon him the bonds of creation; he is bound with us for ever."[2] He is knowledge, power, and action, according to the Upanishads; but his action is the expression of his joy. The singer out of the fulness of his joy sings as the divine singer in joy creates the universe. The Isa Upanishad says: "In the midst of activity alone wilt thou desire to live a hundred years." The state of blessedness is not a lotus land of rest; for worship of God coincides with work for man. In *Gitanjali*, 52, the lover asks: "What is the token left of thy love? It is no flower, no spices, no vase of perfumed water. It is thy mighty sword, flashing as a flame, heavy

[1] Taittiriya Upanishad; see also Brinhadaranyaka Upanishad, iii. 9.

[2] *Gitanjali*, 11.

as a bolt of thunder." So the lover resolves: "From now I leave off all petty decorations. Lord of my heart, no more shall there be for me waiting and weeping in corners, no more coyness and sweetness of demeanour. Thou hast given me thy sword for adornment. No more doll's decorations for me!"[1] With a firm hold on the eternal, the liberated soul sallies forth to meet the adversary, evil, in the world.

But this activity will not be for any selfish interest. In this it resembles children's doings. Children take delight in work, as work with them is not work but effluence, or the outflow of their superfluous energies. Their excess energies find an outlet in play. Nothing sordid or utilitarian enters their will. "He has not learned to despise the dust and hanker after gold."[2] "Pearl fishers dive for pearls, merchants sail in their ships, while children gather pebbles and scatter them again. They seek not for hidden treasures, they know not how to cast nets." The difficulties of the world do not affect them. "Tempest roams in the pathless sky, ships get wrecked in the trackless water, death is abroad and children play."[3] The God-

[1] *Gitanjali*, 52. [2] *Crescent Moon*. [3] *Gitanjali*, 60.

possessed souls are people who, like little children, are innocent, and do work for the mere joy of work, and live for the mere joy of life. "On the seashore of endless worlds is the great meeting of children."[1] The Vedanta system and its latest exponent Rabindranath stand for a synthetic idealism, which while not trying to avoid the temporal and the finite, has still a hold on the Eternal Spirit. They give us a practical mysticism which would have us live and act in the temporal world, but make action a consecration and life a dedication to God. But our work in the temporal world should not absorb all our energies and make us miss the vision universal. With a strong hold on the idea of the all-pervading, we must work in the world. "Oh, grant me my prayer that I may never lose the bliss of the touch of the one in the play of the many."[2] The truly religious hero does the dullest deeds with a singing soul.

VII

The end of man is the realisation of the Self or the infinite in him. This is man's *dharma*. *Dharma* literally means nature, reality, or

[1] *Gitanjali*, 60. [2] *Ibid.* 63.

essence. The essence of man is the infinite. His *dharma* is to become the infinite which he already is in potency. The universal one is the goal of the individual one.

> That is the Supreme Path of This,
> That is the Supreme Treasure of This,
> That is the Supremé World of This,
> That is the Supreme Joy of This.

The divine in us is to be realised. The "That in the This" has to come to its own. The character which distinguishes man from the other species of creation is the presence of the conscious endeavour to free himself from the limits of self and nature and seek for a seat in the kingdom of God. "In man, the life of the animal has taken a further bend. He has come to the beginning of a world, which has to be created by his own will and power."[1] Man is a person. Freedom of endless growth should characterise all his activities. If he fails to do his share of the work in the world of creative freedom, he sins against the Eternal in him. His salvation lies in his freeing his personality from the narrow limitations of selfhood. It is the realisation of the infinite attained by the

[1] *Personality*, p. 88.

surrender of the finite. This giving up of the finite interests dear to man involves pain and suffering, hazard and hardship. The path to realisation, the Katha Upanishad says, is as the sharp edge of a razor.[1] The infinite in man is like the oil in the sesamum seeds, or butter in curds, water in river, or fire in the two pieces of wood.[2] To get oil from sesamum seeds we have to press them, churn the curds before we can have butter, dig the ground for water, and rub the sticks for fire. This is suffering or hardship. Till the goal of the infinite is attained we have risks and dangers. We have to fight with the finite, not physical wars, but spiritual wars. Every moment our finiteness is transcended. It is the nature of the finite or the lower to pass away before the higher arises. The mother who values dearly her charm, grace, and beauty, should sacrifice them all for the higher pleasure of looking upon her firstborn. This pleasure is born in anguish, at the cost of her charm and the peril of her life. It were prettier if we could shake children from trees or reap them from the fields! In Rabindranath's image, "The flower

[1] 3. 14.

[2] Swetaswatara Upanishad, i. 15.

must bring forth the fruit." But when "the time of its fruition arrives . . . it sheds its exquisite petals and a cruel economy compels it to give up its sweet perfume."[1] For the flower to develop, the bud has to die; for the fruit, the flower; for the seed, the fruit; for the plant, the seed. Life is a process of eternal birth and death. Birth is death, and death is birth. All progress is sacrifice. The finite self which has to be transformed into the infinite, which is its destiny, does not easily lend itself to this transformation. We have to lay violent hands on it before we can force it to express the infinite. So long as man is finite, the infinite within him tries to break through the finite. The spirit chafes against the bonds of the flesh. There is ever a striving forward in man to make real the infinite which he already is. The force of the spirit to rid itself of the encumbrances which oppose its free expression, means fight and struggle. The uprush of the infinite, bursting all barriers set up by the finite, means strain and suffering. Till therefore the infinite is reached, the life of the finite individual will be one of strenuous effort and untiring toil, involv-

[1] *Sādhanā*, p. 99.

ing risk and daring, strain and conflict. "The pain was great when the strings were being tuned, my Master!"[1] To suffer pain is the sign of our finiteness. It is the right of man. It is "our true wealth as imperfect beings. . . . It is the hard coin which must be paid for everything valuable in this life, for our power, our wisdom, our love. In pain is symbolised the infinite possibility of perfection, the eternal unfolding of joy."[2] Struggle, therefore, is the world's supreme blessing. Man is born for it as he reaches his aim through it.

To Rabindranath, imperfection is not the sign of a fall from the high estate but a condition of progress to it. It is a matter of gratification that the world is imperfect.

> None lives for ever, brother, and nothing lasts for long. Keep that in mind and rejoice.
>
> Beauty is sweet to us, because she dances to the same fleeting tune with our lives.
>
> Knowledge is precious to us, because we shall never have time to complete it.[3]

But this does not mean that the Absolute is imperfect; for Rabindranath says: "All is

[1] *Fruit-Gathering*, XLIX.; see also *Personality*, p. 103.

[2] *Sādhanā*, pp. 64-65.

[3] *The Gardener*, 68; see also 73.

done and finished in the eternal Heaven."[1] As the sun has spots, and the mountain chasms, so the Absolute has imperfection; but the whole is perfect and sublime. Imperfection is a necessary factor in the universe. It is as real as the created universe itself. A universe without imperfection will be a static, unprogressive blank. But imperfection is not the last thing. It is not the end in itself. It exists only to be overcome in the perfect. As the unreal is the incomplete, so the imperfect is the partial. "Imperfection is not a negation of perfectness; finitude is not contradictory to infinity: they are but completeness manifested in parts, infinity revealed within bounds."[2] Were imperfection the last thing in the universe, then the earth would be no place for human beings to live in. Nirvana, in the crude sense of death or destruction of self, would be the goal of man.[3]

The false view which makes imperfection the last thing, is due to an inadequate understanding of the place of evil and imperfection in the world. If we detach the facts from their setting in the whole, they would look

[1] *The Gardener*, 68. [2] *Sādhanā*, p. 48. [3] *Ibid.* p. 71.

awry and unintelligible. "Only when we detach one individual fact of death, do we see its blankness and become dismayed. We lose sight of the wholeness of life of which death is part." The perfect sacrifice of the cross by itself meant death and persecution, but it contained a spiritual fact which shone out in the darkness and overcame it, the triumph of spirit over death. The physical event enables us to give up the body as a last offering to God. It is the last tribute on earth to be paid to the whole. In death the very being of the finite self is cancelled. Thus if we look at death in its setting, it loses its sting and the grave its victory. Death becomes the messenger of God.[1] In the present war the surface appearances may make one despair of humanity. God's image, man, is torn to shreds and pieces. But if we, without being led away by first appearances, take a calm and balanced view, we shall see in this war not merely the throes of death and disease, but the birth-pangs of a new internationalism based on self-sacrifice and disinterestedness. Hitherto civilisation has based itself on cannibalism.

[1] *Gitanjali*, 86.

"Whenever some ancient civilisation fell into decay and died, it was owing to causes which produced callousness of heart and led to the cheapening of man's worth; when either the state or some powerful group of men began to look upon the people as a mere instrument of their power; when by compelling weaker races to slavery and trying to keep them down by every means, man struck at the foundation of his greatness, his own love of freedom and fair-play. Civilisation can never sustain itself upon cannibalism in any form. For that by which alone man is true can only be nourished by love and justice."[1] We trust, as a result of this war, that the vogue of the philosophy which makes man a machine, and interprets civilisation in terms of mechanics, will give place to a philosophy of spirit and a civilisation based on love and justice. We trust that the sacredness of human nature and its right to the opportunities of self-development will be recognised not merely in Europe, but in the whole world. We refuse to believe that the desolation and madness of Europe have no other ends than themselves. The war,

[1] *Sādhanā*, pp. 111-112.

according to Rabindranath's philosophy, has come to point out the unstable mechanical nature of the existing civilisation and prepare the way for a more spiritual one.

What is the place of suffering in the world? Rabindranath tells us that the individual suffers whenever his desires are not satisfied. But he does not care to know whether his desires represent the needs of his real being, or those of his selfish nature. He is really helped by God's refusal of the many desires of his superficial self: "Day by day thou art making me worthy of thy full acceptance by refusing me ever and anon, saving me from perils of weak, uncertain desire."[1] In Rabindranath Tagore we also come across passages where he makes out that the suffering and misfortune of the world are the opportunities employed by God to draw man's attention to his real destiny.

> Misery knocks at thy door, and her message is that thy lord is wakeful, and he calls thee to the love-tryst through the darkness of night.[2]
>
> When desire blinds the mind with delusion and dust, O thou holy one, thou wakeful, come with thy light and thunder.[3]

---

[1] *Gitanjali*, 14; see also *Fruit-Gathering*, LXXXV.

[2] *Gitanjali*, 27.

[3] *Ibid.* 36.

> The rain has held back for days and days, my God, in my arid heart. The horizon is fiercely naked—not the thinnest cover of a soft cloud, not the vaguest hint of a distant cool shower.
>
> Send thy angry storm, dark with death, if it is thy wish, and with lashes of lightning startle the sky from end to end.[1]

It is out of love that God sends us suffering. "God says to man, 'I heal you therefore I hurt, love you therefore punish.'"[2] In *The King of the Dark Chamber*, Sudharshana feels that the very possibility of union with God has become unthinkable to her on account of her sin. But her lord says: "It will be possible in time . . . the utter and bleak blackness that has to-day shaken you to your soul with fear, will one day be your solace and salvation. What else can my love exist for?"[3] Compare with this, "Whom the Lord loveth, He chasteneth." He gives us "stripes, that would cleanse away evil." Pain and trouble purify the soul. The metal shines the brightest when it passes through the furnace, *e.g.*, love will be all mirth and jollity, without any seriousness, if it runs perfectly smooth. "Love must be called from its play to drink sorrow

[1] *Gitanjali*, 40. [2] *Stray Birds*, 63. [3] *Dark Chamber*, p. 111.

and be borne to the heaven of tears."[1] Love will be the "cold apathy of death," unless there are blows of pain in it.[2] And applying his doctrine, Rabindranath says that the Western soul, which is being deadened by greed and materialism, can be delivered from its present sin and weakness only by suffering. To the interviewer of *Evening Wisconsin*, an American paper, Rabindranath said: "Only by suffering and sorrow shall you be freed from your crushing load. I do not know in what form it will come to you, but it is the only way. Only by great suffering and terrible humiliation shall you be made whole."[3] Suffering is not only the penalty but also the sign of man's disobedience of God's laws. The whole universe is ordered by the divine immanent reason. Destiny is no blind power, but providence. God is, no doubt, a loving God of mercy, but He is also a God of justice. His love expresses itself by means of laws. As He does not break His laws for the sake of His suppliant, He seems hard and pitiless.[4]

[1] *The Gardener*, 68. [2] *Fruit-Gathering*, XXXVIII.

[3] *Modern Review*, 1917, p. 372.

[4] Cf. "Tell thy sins to Him who is most just, being pitiless, most pitiful, being just too" (Oscar Wilde, *A Florentine Tragedy*).

"No one has ever been able to move him."[1] In the same strain Surangama says: "May he ever remain hard and relentless like rock—may my tears and prayers never move him!"[2]

VIII

Sin is selfishness. It is the failure of man to be true to his real self. It is the revolt against the spirit in man, the divine in him. It is the rejection of the all. "It is our desires that limit the scope of our self-realisation, hinder our extension of consciousness, and give rise to sin, which is the innermost barrier that keeps us apart from our God, setting up disunion and the arrogance of exclusiveness. For sin is not one mere action, but it is an attitude of life which takes for granted that our goal is finite, that our self is the ultimate truth, and that we are not all essentially one but exist each for his own separate individual existence."[3] Evil is the assertion of the false independence of the self. It is the antagonism of the individual to the world-whole, which is the ground and truth of the individual self. It is

[1] *Dark Chamber*, p. 129. [2] *Dark Chamber*, p. 129.
[3] *Sādhāna*, p. 111.

the assertion of the superficial self against his true self. It represents the division of self against self, the self which is his shadow against the self which is his reality. "What you are you do not see, what you see is your shadow."[1] Egotism is the root-cause of evil. When selfish standards are set up, distinctions between mine and thine are introduced; man becomes a slave to the fancied goods of wealth and property, not objects of real worth but phantoms raised by the selfish imagination.

> I came out alone on my way to my tryst. But who is this that follows me in the silent dark?
>
> I move aside to avoid his presence but I escape him not.
>
> He makes the dust rise from the earth with his swagger; he adds his loud voice to every word that I utter.
>
> He is my own little self, my lord, he knows no shame; but I am ashamed to come to thy door in his company.[2]

Our selfish desires are our fetters, and our possessions our limitations.[3] "The mist is like the earth's desire. It hides the sun for whom she cries."[4] Selfishness is the mist which obscures our vision and makes us forget

[1] *Stray Birds*, 18. [2] *Gitanjali*, 30.
[3] See *Gitanjali*, 7, 8, 9, and 29; and *Fruit-Gathering*, XI.
[4] *Stray Birds*, 94.

our true being. In our selfishness we think that finite objects can satisfy the infinite craving within. When we seek false ends we become bound by our desires.[1] Our real needs are not satisfied by what we come to possess. There is still the burden weighing on the heart, still the thirst for God, the hunger for the infinite and the transcendent. This is a sign of our finiteness and impotence. We really seek the good, but in our ignorance mistake the wrong thing for the good. Evil as evil is no man's aim. Through ignorance and selfishness we believe the path to blessedness lies in the possession of riches. We cannot imagine the degree to which man is materialised. He goes to the ends of earth to heap up riches. He gets it, but is not contented. No man with a soul in him can find consolation in money or the things that it can buy. The Katha Upanishad says: "No man can be satisfied by riches alone." At the present day this is forgotten, and the one thing that interests us is how to grow rich or make fortune at a stroke. It matters little if other people go under in this rush and hurry for

[1] See *Gitanjali*, 31.

money-making, if the path trodden by this money madness is strewn by numberless victims. Man fancies that he is enjoying himself in the boundless welter and confusion which result when self conflicts with self and spirit is crushed under matter. But those who gain wealth are as miserable as ever. They vie with one another in the huge wealth of their summer palaces, the cost of their motor buses, and the high prices of their wines. The scramble for the good things of the world may go on till the crack of doom, but the soul will not be satisfied. Peace and quiet will be still distant, the bliss of repose unknown, the vexations of the spirit unquenched. Man has aims which do not perish at death. Were he completely material, he could be satisfied by matter. In man there is the undying essence of spirit "that triumphs over Time, and is and will be when time shall be no more."[1] His soul cannot be satisfied by matter. "The tragedy of human life consists in our vain attempts to stretch the limits of things which can never become unlimited,—to reach the infinite by absurdly adding to the

[1] Carlyle.

rungs of the ladder of the finite."[1] The need of the soul is for infinite satisfaction, but so long as it is finite and selfish, so long as it sets itself against the world, the ideal cannot be reached. The self will always be limited by what is outside it. It may go on acquiring objects in an endless manner, but is no better after the conquest of the world than before it. The limit is still there. Acquisition of objects has only resulted in the added pain of weariness. Pessimism is the result. Schopenhauer is right in holding that the asserting of the individual in his exclusive individuality only increases his misery. The way out of this condition is for the individual to give up his exclusiveness through devotion to an end beyond himself. If human nature is so limited that the absorption into a larger end is impossible for it, then the fate of man is pitiable indeed. In that case, an intelligible ethic, logic, and metaphysic will all become impossible. Incidentally, Rabindranath refers to the misfortune which is overtaking India. While the West is waking up to the enormity of the defect, India is fast falling a prey to it. She is slowly

[1] *Sādhanā*, pp. 150-151.

exchanging her ideals of spirit and indifference to material conditions for those of materialism and enjoyment. The educated classes with their fear of poverty and rush for gold are the worst sinners in this respect. They are on the inclined plane which leads to loss of life and destruction of spirit. Many are living on the edge of a precipice, and more are breaking down from the strain of the pursuit of pelf and place. Certainly the world is suffering from a fell disease. He is not wrong who said that the world was suffering from appendicitis. Those favoured by fortune in this competition for wealth have only a cynical smile for men of Rabindranath's type who devote their attention to spiritual things.

> Men going home glance at me and smile and fill me with shame. I sit like a beggar maid, drawing my skirt over my face, and when they ask me, what it is I want, I drop my eyes and answer them not.[1]

> Those who have everything but thee, my God, laugh at those who have nothing but thyself.[2]

No man can gain immortality by wealth, says the Upanishad. Wealth is only a means and not an end. But when it becomes the

[1] *Gitanjali*, 41. [2] *Stray Birds*, 226.

end, and when it is in the saddle and rides mankind, man is degraded. For when man makes his weapons his gods and "when his weapons win he is defeated himself."[1] The mind of man cast in the spiritual mould should not sink to the worship of the golden image. That cannot satisfy its real longing. Our prayer should be: "Master, give me the least fraction of the wealth that disdains all the wealth of the world."[2]

What is true of individuals is true of nations. Selfishness here too is the root of evil. Patriotism devoid of considerations of humanity is nothing but selfishness on a larger scale. The individual wants wealth, the nation wants earth. In both cases it is greed and hunger for matter. Imperialism is nothing but selfishness enlarged and nationalised. It is the outcome of selfish nationalism. It is an organised form of human greed and avarice. Alas! that nations should measure their greatness by their material wealth and extent of territory! They are not satisfied when their ambitions are reached. Alexander the Great sighed that

[1] *Stray Birds*, 45. [2] *Fruit-Gathering*, XXVII.

there were no more worlds to conquer. The war which is deluging Europe with blood points the same moral. The European nations have got all they wanted; all the good things of the earth, trade ports, etc., are theirs. They have lived unto themselves; grown rich beyond their dreams at other people's cost, and lacked nothing, and still they worry. There is no end to their ambition. We find them burning with the fever of acquiring new possessions, rushing to and fro like maddened animals stung by gadflies. "It is an endlessly wearisome task, this continual adding to our stores."[1] Satisfaction of the infinite cannot be reached by a summation of finites. The larger the outward acquisition, the greater the inner discontent. In the sea they feel thirst. There is water everywhere, but there is not a drop to drink. The Western nations forget God and walk other ways. They deny brotherhood both in their national organisations and international relations. Rabindranath points to the essential defect of the Western civilisation in these words: "You people over here seem to be all in a

[1] *Sādhanā*, p. 147.

state of continual strife. It is all struggling, hard striving to live. There is no place for rest, or peace of mind, or that meditative relief which in our country we feel to be needed, for the health of our spirits." Speaking about the atmosphere of the tabernacle where the preacher, Mr. Billy Sunday, lectures, it is said: "It is the atmosphere of the circus rather than of the church. There is more entertainment in the tabernacle than there is theology. . . . As one young man put it, 'I don't go to the movies now—I go to the tabernacle. It's more fun, and it doesn't cost me anything.'"[1] When the house of prayer becomes a centre of gaiety, church-going the short cut to sensation, and religion amusement, it only shows how low and frivolous the mind of man has become. Even Western critics noticed this defect. We have Edward Carpenter's cure for the disease of modern civilisation. Matthew Arnold noticed this weakness in these terms:

> We glance and nod and hurry by,
> And never once possess our souls
> Before we die.

---

[1] Dr. Mulford in the *Outlook*, 18th April 1917, p. 706.

Life in the West is one long fever and struggle which know neither rest nor pause in the breathless rush and hurry for sensation and excitement, possession and conquest. It believes that mere movement is life, and that the more velocity it has, the more it expresses vitality.[1]

IX

Being and becoming, stillness and strife, are inseparable aspects of reality. The Absolute includes harmony and peace as much as strain and tension. While the Westerner does not care for being or stillness, he is absorbed in the world of becoming and strife. "It is because of this insistence on the doing and the becoming that we perceive in the west the intoxication of power."[2] Mr. G. Lowes Dickinson remarks: "All America is Niagara—force without direction, noise without significance, speed without accomplishment." To the Westerns Rabindranath's advice is not to live sensationally. Love of novelty and sensation ought not to be the principle of life. The West, giddy with its

[1] Tagore's message to the women of America, *Current Opinion*, April 1917.

[2] *Sādhanā*, p. 126.

conquest over matter, needs periods of rest and contemplation. "In our country the danger comes from the opposite side."[1] We lay stress on the being aspect. We do not care for the world of becoming, and so have the "intoxication of the spirit." The pervading concern for the things of the spirit has led to an unconcern for the things of the world, and we are to-day reaping the fruits of age-long unconcern and other-worldliness. We have never cared to provide for the great masses of our population the necessary conditions of material existence, indispensable to civilised life. Here we have much to learn from the West. Rabindranath is equally vehement against the Western feeding of the flesh which starves the soul and the Eastern saving of the soul which slays the body. An integral harmony of the two is the ideal. A balanced *attitude* towards life demands leisure and solitude for thought and contemplation as well as work in the world. Random busyness as well as complete renunciation is a failure to live the life of man. We have to choose *both* the calm of contemplation and the

[1] *Sādhanā*, p. 126.

stress of life, the joy of self-abandonment and the pride of creativity, and not either. "But true spirituality, as taught in our sacred lore, is calmly balanced in strength, in the correlation of the within and the without."[1] Rabindranath is not unworldly in the sense that he has a contempt for the world, though the things of the world are treated by him as of little moment when compared with the things of the soul. He has no patience with those who wish to give the slip to life. "You love to discover that I love this world where you have brought me."[2] He calls upon the mystical souls of India, the unpractical dreamers with no strength for action, to become apostles of work and social idealism. He who holds back from the work of the world is like him who runs away from battle. Life is no rest but a game, no parade but a battle. Rabindranath cautions us not to lose ourselves in reverie, but face facts and fight the battles of life. To the Indian ascetic Rabindranath's advice is: "Come out of thy meditations and leave aside thy flowers and incense! What harm is there if thy clothes

[1] *Sādhanā*, p. 127.

[2] *Fruit-Gathering*, LXXV.

become tattered and stained? Meet him and stand by him in toil and in sweat of thy brow."[1] Of course Rabindranath is aware that "he who is too busy doing good finds no time to be good."[2] He is hard against the patriot of the present-day India who with a self-consciousness bordering on pride goes about slumming as slumming is the fashion, organising meetings as that is the way of the world, making speeches as that is the road to preferment. Busybodies who by such social "scavengering" draw a veil over their sickness of soul are really doing an injury to the eternal welfare of India's children. The true worker, who works for the joy of it, does his work so simply and naturally. "From the grasses in the field to the stars in the sky, each one is doing just that."[3] "Either you have work or you have not. When you have to say, 'Let us do something,' then begins mischief."[4] "He who wants to do good knocks at the gate; he who loves finds the gate open."[5] Rabindranath advocates such an utter self-consecration to one's calling

[1] *Gitanjali*, 11.
[2] *Stray Birds*, 184.
[3] Letters: *Modern Review*, May 1917.
[4] *Stray Birds*, 171.
[5] *Ibid.* 83.

that it has become unconscious. For the law of creative action and joy is such that "where man is at his greatest, he is unconscious."[1]

It is only the pursuit of the integral ideal that can satisfy the infinite soul. Anything less than the whole is "false as a mirage, empty as a bubble."[2] It is absurd to see in the part the image of the whole. Sooner or later, the unsatisfying nature of the part will manifest itself. "We must come to an end in our evil doing, in our career of discord. For evil is not infinite, and discord cannot be an end in itself."[3] "Evil cannot altogether arrest the course of life on the highway and rob it of its possessions. For evil has to pass on, it has to grow into good; it cannot stand and give battle to the All." "No littleness can keep us shut up in its walls of untruth for aye."[4] "Mistakes are but the preludes to their own destruction."[5] As error and untruth must break down by the logical inconsistencies and contradictions which are inherent in them, if they are worked out to their consequences, even so evil will be found to conflict with itself, go against its own root-

[1] *Nationalism*, p. 81. [2] *Dark Chamber*, p. 113.
[3] *Sādhanā*, p. 84. [4] *Dark Chamber*, p. 14. [5] *Ibid.* p. 154.

principles, and confess itself inadequate for the aim it is intended to satisfy. Sin must break down against the All. Evil is an attitude which can never be consistently held. Only the infinite can satisfy the soul. "Our heart is restless until it finds its rest in Thee," says Augustine. Nothing else satisfies it. Tauler declares: "The soul's desire is an abyss which cannot be filled except by a good which is infinite." So also Rabindranath: "Away from the sight of thy face my heart knows no rest nor respite." "That I want thee, only thee—let my heart repeat without end. All desires that distract me, day and night, are false and empty to the core."[1] To overcome sin we have to repudiate our exclusiveness and rest our faith firm in the all inclusive whole. The consciousness of man gets its fulfilment when it is merged in the consciousness of God. Religion speaks to us of that love of God in which all our earthly relations are swallowed up. Only in such a relation of soul to God do we have a fruition of our desires. Our souls have rest and repose only in the infinite. This final condition is a state of utter delight or

[1] *Gitanjali*, 5 and 38.

perfect harmony where all discords are overcome, an eternal calm where the unrest of life is stilled. In such a state we have a transvaluation of all values.

> When I think of this end of my moments, the barrier of the moments breaks and I see by the light of death thy world with its careless treasures. Rare is its lowliest seat, rare is its meanest of lives.
>
> Things that I longed for in vain and things that I got—let them pass. Let me but truly possess the things that I ever spurned and overlooked.[1]

Much we call great will lose its greatness. Much we call little will become great. We shall see the worth of man as man, and not rate it according to his wealth. In that kingdom, maybe, the child, the slave, and the harlot take precedence of the learned, the rich, and the king. We shall then recognise the real place of money as the medium of spirit, and matter as the vehicle of mind. We shall know that the things of spirit are real, and in the last resort the only real. The walls which divide man from man will become transparent; selfishness, which is the only sin, will appear to be the pursuit of a phantom. We shall then say, with the Princess in *The King of the Dark*

[1] *Gitanjali*, 38.

Chamber, "Nothing of this is mine, it is all yours, O lord!"[1]

The crucial point of distinction between Western Christianity and Vedantism is found in the relation of God to man. Western Christianity lays stress on man's sinfulness, guilt, and need of salvation by God. If man, who is naturally corrupt, should become transformed into a virtuous soul, it can only be by the influx of divine energy. But Rabindranath does not accept this doctrine of man's natural corruption. "It has been held that sinfulness is the nature of man, and only by the special grace of God can a particular person be saved. This is like saying that the nature of the seed is to remain enfolded within its shell, and it is only by some special miracle that it can be grown into a tree."[2] The barrier between God and man is overthrown in Rabindranath's view as in the Vedanta system. The infinite dwells in man, and that is the glory of manhood. "And my pride is from the life-throb of ages dancing in my blood this moment."[3] The infinite is in man, not in the sense that it is perfectly

[1] Page 199. [2] *Sādhanā*, p. 74. [3] *Gitanjali*, 69.

realised, but in the sense that it is potential in him. Man is but the localised expression of God. The light that lighteth every man that cometh into the world is there though it does not shine through. Progress is the unfolding or the coming out with an ever-increasing and brightening radiance of the perfect light within. For it to shine through, the surrounding ignorance has to be cleared away.

> There is an inmost centre in us all,
> Where truth abides in fulness ; and round
> Wall upon wall, the gross flesh hems it in. . . .
> And to know, rather consists in opening out a way
> Whence the imprisoned splendour may escape,
> Than in effecting entry for a light
> Supposed to be without.

We require a removal of Avidya or ignorance, a breaking of the bonds of Maya or selfishness, and not an ingress of divine spirit from outside as the result of prayer to an offended God who yet loves man and has pity for his frailty. The light is present, wrapped up in a cloud of darkness and selfishness. Sin is the inordinate love of darkness, fancying it to be the real self. The dark and dusty soul believes itself to be enjoying what it refuses to God, to whom it really belongs. It takes delight in its own darkness, and this delight is its death and destruction. The sinful soul believes that the wheels of time move forward for ministering to its needs and comfort. For it, the sun and moon shine, and the trees bring forth their flowers and fruit. When the false self-sufficiency disappears, the scales drop from the eyes and the man is saved. "When I give up the helm I know that the time has come for thee to take it."[1] He then feels that all creation is one with God as the centre. Michael Angelo is reported to have said that every block of marble contained a statue, and the sculptor brought it to light by cutting away the encumbrances by which the "human face divine is concealed." Even so we have to cut away the encumbrances, and remove the obstacles for the expression of the infinite. Deliverance is not by grace, but by the removal of ignorance and selfishness. "In the typical thought of India it is held that the true deliverance of man is the deliverance from *avidyā*, from ignorance. It is not in destroying anything that is positive and real, for that

[1] *Gitanjali*, 99.

cannot be possible, but that which is negative, which obstructs our vision of truth. When this obstruction, which is ignorance, is removed, then only is the eyelid drawn up which is no loss to the eye."[1]

The barrier between God and man according to the Vedantic ideas is not impassable. Man can become as perfect as the father which is in heaven. The Taittiriya Upanishad says: "He who knows Brahma obtains liberation." The Mundaka Upanishad says: "He who knows the supreme Brahman verily becomes Brahman." But the West has never been reconciled to this idea of our unity with the infinite being. "It condemns, as a piece of blasphemy, any implication of man's becoming God." Rabindranath is quite strong on this point. "Yes, we must become Brahma. We must not shrink from avowing this. Our existence is meaningless if we never can expect to realise the highest perfection that there is."[2] "We have known the fulfilment of man's personality in gaining God's nature for itself, in utter self-giving out of abundance of love. Men have been born in this world of nature,

[1] *Sādhanā*, p. 72; see also viii. [2] *Ibid.* pp. 154-155.

with our human limitations and appetites, and yet . . . became one with their God in the free active life of the infinite."[1] No Hindu can accept that what has been possible with Christ is impossible with other men. The perfection Christ attained is what all men might have if they would. God spoke through Christ but as He had spoken through the great men of all ages and countries. When the highest perfection is reached, the rhythm of man's life becomes one with that of the cosmic spirit; his soul then vibrates in perfect accord with the eternal principle.

X

Between the stern philosophy of Sankara with its rigorous logic of negation and the ascetic ethic of inaction, and the human philosophy of Rabindranath Tagore, it is war to the knife. In the centuries of political depression which preceded Sankara's birth, when India was a prey to external invasions and internal anarchy, Buddhism with its gospel of asceticism made a strong appeal to the people of India, who had by then become

[1] *Personality*, p. 106.

weary of existence. According to Buddhism, action is the chief end to be avoided. The highest wisdom consists in withdrawing from the world into the depths of the soul. "To the Buddhist, this world is transitory, vile and miserable; the flesh is a burden, desire an evil, personality a prison."[1] The great joy in existence gives place to an ascetic code. As the people were at strife with the world outside, they courted a religion which bade them seek peace inside. As the Greek in the worst days of his political career was thrown back on his own resources, finding no happiness in the world outside, even so the Hindu exchanged his balanced outlook on life for a one-sided abstract view—an individualism which fights shy of the world with its correlate of *maya* developed. An imperfect estimate of the values of the world was the result. Reflection became the sole end of man, and revolt against the world the means to it. The Indian thought that he should realise freedom by cutting off the encumbrances which made man depend upon the chances of the world, and secure peace in the solitary existence of the

[1] Laurence Binyon, *Painting in the Far East*, p. 22.

self. It was Sankara's task to effect a synthesis, and make out that Hinduism could satisfy even souls trained in Buddhistic principles. We have in the philosophical synthesis left by Sankara a characteristic attempt to combine the central principles of Buddhism and those of the Vedanta religion in one whole. The ancient Indian sages were most at home in the world, and believed in an all-embracing divinity. But Buddhism finds no necessity for God in the world-process. While the ancient sages of India never advocated a withdrawal from the delights of the world, they protested against a life of sense, that of a typical voluptuary. Buddhism holds emancipation from the world to be the supreme end of man. Sankara, without touching the root-principles of Vedantism, grafted on to it the Buddhistic principles of *maya* and monasticism. The Buddhist spoke of the flux of the finite universe, and Sankara admits the world is *maya*. The anxiety to be loyal as far as possible to both Buddhism and Vedantism appears to be the explanation of much of the inconsistency of Sankara's philosophy. God or the Absolute he cannot give up as a

Vedantin. But when, with the Buddhist, he admits that the finite is illusory, his Absolute becomes something in which all is lost and nothing is found again. If change and multiplicity are regarded as unreal, then even permanence becomes reduced to an unreality. But the Vedantic Absolute clings to him, and he rightly views it as pure affirmation or fulness of being. Here and there we come across passages where Sankara holds to the right view of the relation between the world and the Absolute. But these have lost their force, as passages pointing to an opposite view are to be met with in almost every page of Sankara's writings, and as the interpreters of Sankara's system have practically ignored it. But there is no denying that the positive method Sankara intends to pursue as a Vedantin and the negative method he does sometimes pursue as an interpreter of Buddhism, end in conflict and contradiction.

Since Buddhism disturbed the old balanced outlook of the Aryan mind two thousand years ago, there has been a revolt of spirit against matter in India. After Buddhism became practically extinct in the soil, the school of

Sankara has kept the flame alive. Though Buddhism as a distinct sect disappeared from the land of its birth, the lessons of Buddhism remained an essential part of the religious teaching of India; for in the general evolution of Hindu philosophy the principles of Buddhism were assimilated by the Hindu doctrine. They got merged in the main current of Indian thought. A noble band of saints and sages, of sacred memory, have lived up to this ideal, sternly rebuking all contact with the sense-world, and stoutly refusing to live the life of the world. The ancient wisdom of India held renunciation to be only a factor and not the end in itself. The balanced harmony between the great affirmation and the great renunciation is emphasised by the humanist thinkers of the country. Rabindranath Tagore is the representative of the humanist school. The impression that Rabindranath's views are different from those of Hinduism is due to the fact that Hinduism is identified with a particular aspect of it—Sankara Vedanta, which, on account of historical accidents, turned out a world-negating doctrine. Rabindranath 's religion is identical with the ancient wisdom of the Upanishads, the Bhagavadgita, and the theistic systems of a later day.

Our conclusion is that in his *Sādhanā* and other works, Rabindranath, by his power of imagination, has breathed life into the dry bones of the ancient philosophy of India and made it live. His teaching is in no sense a mere borrowed product of Christianity; indeed, it goes deeper in certain fundamental aspects than Christianity as represented to us in the West. And if Rabindranath's religion is something "better than the Christianity which came into it,"[1] it only shows that the ancient religion of India has not much to gain from Western Christianity.

[1] *Quarterly Review*, October 1914.

CHAPTER III

POETRY AND PHILOSOPHY

> He spoke of poetry, and how
> Divine it was—a light, a love—
> A spirit which like wind doth blow
> As it listeth, to and fro.
> A dew rained down from God above;
> A power which comes and goes like dream,
> And which none can ever trace—
> Heaven's light on earth—Truth's brightest beam.
>
> SHELLEY.

More and more mankind will discover that we have to turn to poetry to interpret life for us, to console us, to sustain us. Without poetry, our science will appear incomplete, and most of what now passes with us for religion and philosophy will be replaced by poetry. . . . The day will come when we shall wonder at ourselves for having trusted to them, for having taken them seriously; and the more we perceive their hollowness, the more we shall prize "the breath and finer spirit of knowledge" offered to us by poetry.—MATTHEW ARNOLD.

I

IN Chapter I., Section I., we have said that Rabindranath is essentially a poet and not a philosopher, though it is possible for us to gather his philosophical views from his poetry. There are critics who consider Rabindranath's poetry not to be first-rate, because it is full of metaphysics and mysticism. The first two chapters dealing with the philosophical teaching of Rabindranath only strengthen the suspicion, and leave the reader in genuine doubt about the worth of Rabindranath's poetry. His departure from the conventions of poetic form adds to the difficulties and helps to make the suspicion gather in weight and become well-nigh certain. Let us here consider how far the criticism is just, and incidentally notice Rabindranath's views about the relation of poetry to philosophy, and topics of a kindred nature.

II

The question to be decided at the outset relates to the aim of art, especially poetic art. In *The Cycle of Spring*, Rabindranath says: "We [poets] set men free from their desires."[1] In these words he lays his finger on the true function of art as the pathway to freedom.

[1] Page 18.

The artist helps us to forget the bonds with the world, and reveals to us the invisible connections by which we are bound up with eternity. True art withdraws our thoughts from the mere machinery of life, and lifts our souls above the meanness of it. It releases the self from the restless activities of the world, and takes us out "of the noisy sick-room of ourselves." It disengages the mind from its imprisonment in the web of customary associations and routine ideas. The secret of all art lies in self-forgetfulness. The poet or the artist sets free the poet or the artist in us. And this he can do only if his artistic creation is born of self-forgetful joy. The true artist lifts himself above all worldly passions and desires, into the spiritual mood where he waits for the light. He turns away from all other objects, identifies himself with the particular subject he wishes to interpret, merges his consciousness in it, and loses himself. He calls out to the object whose beauty he wishes to be revealed:

> . . . Be thou, Spirit fierce,
> My spirit! be thou me, impetuous one.[1]

---

[1] Shelley.

When this forgetfulness of self and identification with the not-self occurs, when the life within the artist becomes one with the life without him, art takes its birth. It is because art is born of this joy that it produces joy. When we say that the function or aim of art is to produce enjoyment, it is not to be understood that either the artist, or the creator, or the enjoying man starts with any conscious purpose to delight or the deliberate design to enjoy. Artistic creation and enjoyment are both spontaneous and unconscious. The artist does not create his work with any specific motive of pleasing the audience or delighting the world. What is felt deeply in the soul of the artist finds outward shape in the work of art. Out of the fulness of the heart the mouth speaketh. "The road of excess leads to the palace of wisdom," says William Blake. Art has its origin, according to Rabindranath, "in the region of the superfluous."[1] The surplus energy seeks its outlet in art. Art is the daughter of joy. It is due to play, the expression of the superfluous energies of man. Man speaks with his voice when he has a

[1] *Personality*, p. 10

purpose to gain; but when he has none such, he sings. He walks with his feet when he has an end to reach, but when he has none such, he dances. Man writes with his hand, and works with it when he has an axe to grind, but when he has none such, he paints with it. But if all our time and energies are taken up by war and trade, science and industry, then we cannot afford to waste our precious time and energies in painting and chiselling, singing and dancing! Our society will have no place for those idlers, we mean the artists! But art is born of idle-ness, and not busy-ness. In art we do not seek for the fulfilment of our physical or intellectual needs. We only feel and enjoy, but do not analyse or measure. Repetition of facts that can be turned to use and advantage, such as "the sun is round, water is liquid, fire is hot, would be intolerable. But a description of the beauty of the sunrise," which has absolutely no economic or utilitarian value, will have "its eternal interest . . . because there, it is not the fact of the sunrise, but its relation to ourselves, which is the object of perennial interest."[1] Art deals with

[1] *Personality*, p. 15.

the world of personality. Art is the expression of personality. But it may be argued that all activity is self-expression, and so, to say that art is self-expression does not go far. But we have to remember that everywhere else, activity is a means to something else, while in beauty we have no ulterior aim.

We want to know a thing that we may use it. In art, self-expression has no other end. It is its own object. Self-expression occurs because it cannot but occur. It is not to satisfy any physical or economic needs. "When our heart is fully awakened in love, or in other great emotions, our personality is in its flood-tide."[1] Poetry is not work, but an outburst, or an effluence as Browning puts it. It is the expression of the excess where the whole soul comes out. As art is born of the joy of self-forgetfulness it fulfils the aim of delighting, or producing joy, and thus helps the soul to leap free of its fetters and attain peace with itself and the world. It lifts us up into a mood where everything actual becomes practically nothing. It helps the soul to enter its own natural home, and claim its citizenship in that

[1] *Personality*, p. 17.

kingdom of freedom and beauty where all are sovereigns and none subjects. At the same time it affects the greater life of which it is a part; for it brings the infinite into the common life. It thus adorns life and gladdens existence.

Art is not didactic. It is to delight and not to instruct. It is to stimulate us unconsciously to noble ends and not to teach lessons. Philosophy may argue and instruct; religion may exhort and command; but art only delights and pleases. Instruction and edification may be the results of art, but its aim is only to delight. While it shines by its own light, the light may produce other effects. As a species of art, the aim of poetry is to please and not profit.

The popular notion that Indian thought is not in sympathy with this conception of the aim of art is a mistake. "The rhetoricians in old India had no hesitation in saying, that enjoyment is the soul of literature,—the enjoyment which is disinterested."[1] When delight, the aim of art, is confused with pleasure interpreted in the vulgar hedonistic sense, then

[1] *Personality*, p. 8.

Indian thought enters its emphatic protest. When art caters to our craze for sensation, it is criticised and condemned. The ascetic note in India is the expression of the revolt against, not the spiritual aim of art, but the hedonistic degradation of that aim. The æsthetic emotion is a spiritual experience and not a mere subjective feeling. When art ceases to be a means of attaining spiritual freedom, and becomes merely the occasion for the amusement of the vulgar, it has forfeited its true nature as art.

III

Though it is not the aim of poetry as a species of art to tell us of a philosophy, still it cannot fulfil its purpose unless it embodies a philosophic vision. It must offer an interpretation of life, give us a fuller view of reality. Poetry would not delight and give joy if it did not reveal the eternal through its form. Poetry aims, in the language of Hegel, "to present in forms for the imagination features of the ultimate ideal of the harmonised universe." Aristotle has said that poetry is the most philosophic of all writing, as its object is truth. The true poet is he who sees the whole in every part and makes his poetry express his whole vision. "The chief office of poetry is not merely to give amusement, not merely to be the expression of feelings good or bad of mankind, or to increase our knowledge of human nature, and of human life, but that, if it includes this mission, it also includes a mission far higher, the revelation, namely, of ideal truth, the revelation of that world of which this world is but the shadow or the drossy copy, the revelation of the eternal, the unchanging and the typical which underlies the unsubstantial and the ever-dissolving phenomena of earth's empire of matter and time."[1] Poetry should give us a vision of the whole. We may well say that one of the decisive tests to help us to find out whether a particular work is poetry or not is this, whether it gives us a wholeness of vision or reads only the surface appearances. Instead, therefore, of saying that philosophy and poetry are incompatible, we should say that poetry to be poetry must be essentially philosophical, in the sense here explained.

[1] Churton Collins, *The True Function of Poetry*.

For it is only a mind that is at rest, a soul at peace with itself, that can produce good poetry. A disturbed soul or a worried mind cannot be a great poet. It is the rhythm of life that expresses itself in the rhythm of poetry. There will be melody in the tongue only if there is melody in the heart. The harmony of the soul is attained when the mind is not seized with doubts. It is only then that the soul sinks into a kind of passivity, surrenders itself to the spontaneity of creation, and finds its joy therein. The human soul to rise into poetic rapture should become attuned with the soul of things beyond. The inner and the outer self must melt into one sweet harmony. "This world, whose soul seems to be aching for expression in its endless rhythm of lines and colours, music and movements, hints and whispers, and all the suggestion of the inexpressible, finds its harmony in the ceaseless longing of the human heart to make the Person manifest in its own creations."[1] It is the universal joy that takes shape in the song of the poet. Poetry is the echo in the human heart of the melody of the universe. A

[1] *Personality*, pp. 32-33.

soul ill at ease with the world, which thinks that the world is given up for lost, as God is confined to His heaven, cannot be a great poet. The pessimist who sees an irreconcilable breach between the higher and the lower, the transcendentalist who looks upon the ideal as something beyond time and the world-process, and the world-negating ascetic who longs to fly from this life into nothingness, these cannot be great poets, as they are at war with the world. Pessimistic poetry is a contradiction in terms; for he who finds nothing valuable in this world cannot be a poet. The true poet finds his happiness in the world or not at all. The poet must have love of nature and of creation. Rabindranath thus describes the relation of the artist soul to the world soul: "The world asks the inner man,—'Friend, have you seen me? Do you love me?—not as one who provides you with foods and fruits, not as one whose laws you have found out, but as one who is personal, individual?' The artist's answer is, 'Yes, I have seen you, I have loved and known you,—not that I have any need of you, not that I have taken you and used your laws for my own purposes of power. I know the forces that act and drive and lead to power, but it is not that. I see you, where you are what I am.' "[1] Disinterested love for the universe, as it is only a revelation of one's own soul, is the true artist's attitude to the world. A poet who wishes to see beauty everywhere must love the earth. The soul must be at home in the world and feel no strangeness in it. It must cry out, "Is not this earth also His who made heaven?"[2] The true poet hears harmony in the babel of sounds called nature, sees good in the heart of evil, and views eternity in time. The disturbances of the soul and the antinomies of the world do not make him think that God is either non-existent, or, if existent, has gone stark mad, but only strengthen his world-view in its wholeness. Of course he would feel ugliness and evil like pain. "When they had struck thee and thou wert pained, it pierced me to the quick."[3] But in all true poetry as in all true philosophy, the end must be reconciliation. The poet may display his art in describing the tragic contrasts of the world, but

[1] *Personality*, p. 22. [2] *Fruit-Gathering*, LV. [3] *Ibid.*

he is convinced that the end of it all is peace and atonement, and not discord and despair. This does not mean that the fifth scene of the fifth act should be one of marriage or benediction. Nor does it mean that he should view the world as a pure paradise without any conflicts and contrasts. The poet should face the world with its ugliness and misery, horror and imperfection, but in the end let us feel that the world we live in is good enough. He may describe the tumult of the soul, but only to conclude that underneath it there is a settled peace. Pure and ennobling are the effects of great tragedies which describe the agonies of soul and the groanings of spirit. A tragedy which leaves on the mind an impression of disgust and dissatisfaction is a failure as a work of art. The ultimate feeling in true art should be one of triumph and satisfaction. The tragedy is an illustration of the law of the universal in the particular, and exhibits the realisation of the whole in the sorrows of the individuals. Any other course would be to give up the rationality of the beauty of the universe. The dull world may have discords and contradictions, but the world of poetry which is nature idealised cannot contain them. Roughly speaking, only partial views, which are the monopoly of science and prose, can consider contradiction the end of things. To them the world may appear an interrogation, but to the philosopher and the poet it cannot be so. Their task is to show that conflict and confusion are not the last thing. They make a perfect round of the broken arcs of the earth. The beauty and order of the world are recreated alike in the vision of the poet and the mind of the philosopher. The philosopher argues that all discord is harmony not understood; the poet shows us the soul of goodness in things evil. The eternal harmony of the world is heard in the song of the poet. "My poet, is it thy delight to see thy creation through my eyes and to stand at the portals of my ears silently to listen to thine own eternal harmony?"[1]

IV

On this view the naturalistic conception of poetry stands self-condemned. As art is distinct from nature, so is naturalistic poetry

[1] *Gitanjali*, 65.

distinct from true poetry. The former requires mere observation, while the latter demands meditation on the material observed. While in the former our mind is in a relatively passive condition, in the latter it is in an active state, reflecting on the data observed. As philosophy is not common sense but a criticism thereof, even so poetry is not life but a criticism of it. As philosophy does not catalogue facts but reduces them to law and order, even so poetry does not copy facts but interprets them. Philosophy, by revealing the deeper meanings of things, criticises the superficial appearances, and the poet sets against the ugly show of things their inner spiritual beauty. Philosophy according to the idealist tradition is a construction of experience. The immediate facts of the world, which constitute the starting-point of the philosophic inquiry, are taken up into a synthesis where their immediacy and externality are broken down. Even so the imagination of the poet plays with the facts of the world and makes them express the spirit of the whole. Poetry is not therefore an unimaginative copying of life and matter. The aim of the poet is to reveal the life within things, the soul within matter. The philosopher tells us that mechanism is not the ultimate category of the universe, while the poet sees the life in things which pass for dead. As truth is no mere correspondence to fact, so poetry is no mere imitation of the facts of nature or the flow of mind. Both are creative reconstructions. Both are mirrors of life, not of life at its surface, but of life at its deepest and the best side. If poetry consists in putting down exactly what we see without wavering, as some of our modern poets do when they sing of the kerosene tin and the telegraph wire, it is not true poetry. Beauty is truth, as Keats observed, and not naturalism. Poetry is creation, not copying. It is vision, not imitation. It is picture, not photograph. Indian thought never cared for nature divorced from spirit. Nature thus viewed is an illusive phenomenon. It is real as revealing the divine essence or spirit. Art is the effort of the human mind to grasp the spiritual meaning and inner beauty of the facts of nature. Things of the world are not beautiful by themselves; but as containing suggestions of things above, they are beautiful. But when poetry attempts to photograph things it ceases to be poetry, and becomes prose or science, or something else. Poetry must attach greater importance to the inner informing spirit than to the outward semblance. Fidelity, not to nature but to the soul in it, is the principle of true poetry. So while it is right to say that poetry should be the expression of feeling, it should not be the expression of subjective or individual feeling. It should be the utterance of the universal mind or the general will. It should express feeling lit by reflection. As every natural fact is presented to us in the light of its ideal aim, so every subjective feeling should be given out as an illustration of the poet's whole experience. In poetry not merely a particular emotion, but the poet's whole perception should be released. Every feeling should be given out as an item of the poet's whole vision, which is the inspiration of the poet's work. Rabindranath writes: "Poetry is not a mere matter of feeling or expression, it is the creation of form. Ideas take on shape by some hidden subtle skill at work within the poet. This creative power is the origin of poetry. Sensations, feelings, or language are only its raw material."[1] True poetry will be a compound of emotion and reflection. Mere feeling or emotion will have no voice or utterance. It would be speechless as subjectivism in philosophy is. Without restraint of feeling by thought there would be no realisation, and so no poetry. "The creation of beauty is not the work of unbridled imagination. Passion when it is given its full sway becomes a destructive force like fire gone out of hand."[2] This is Wordsworth's meaning when he says that poetry is emotion remembered in tranquillity. The simplicity of the poetic garb sometimes misleads us into thinking that poetry is only the expression of a surface feeling; but spontaneity and simplicity are in inverse proportion to the training and thought involved. "That training is the most intricate which leads to the utter simplicity of a tune."[3] Poetry is not to be put down for a relaxation of our powers or a detention of our faculties. It involves much strenuous exertion and critical reflection. When the powers of man are at the highest, we feel as if they

[1] Letters, *Modern Review*, August 1917.

[2] *Modern Review*, September 1911, p. 226.

[3] *Gitanjali*, 12.

were at the lowest. It is similar to the optical illusion where both motion and motionlessness seem one. The artist lives a more intense life than the common folk; for only of intensity is insight born.

The transcendental view, which makes poetry, as distinct from prose, deal with ideals which have no reality in life, is at the opposite extreme to the naturalistic view, and is equally abstract and unreal. The classical poet, who "as a swimmer without the impediments of garments cleaves the water with greater ease," constructs a dream world or a fairy land, neglecting the pain and suffering inherent in life, is at the opposite pole to the realistic poet, who pictures the world as it strikes the retina of his eye, and gives us a photograph of the world at its surface. To say that poetry is unrelated to life is as incorrect as to say that poetry is a mere imitation of life. To the poet, earth is his home and heaven his hope. A true philosophy tells us that the distinctions between the actual and the ideal, nature and art, life and criticism, and observation and reflection are relative. The two become opposed when we draw a hard-and-fast line of distinction between the surface view of things, which we call the natural, and the deeper one which penetrates the veil, which we call the philosophical. But art is merely nature deeply felt and meditated upon. "The art itself is nature."[1] The naturalistic and the transcendental views of poetry, which consider that poetry should deal with surface facts or abstract ideals, correspond to the two extreme positions in philosophy, represented by naturalistic realism and transcendental idealism. These have for their counterparts in ethics, hedonism in the utilitarian sense, and rationalism in the ascetic sense. All these are one-sided. True philosophy teaches us that the whole consists of ideals permeating actualities. The real is the rational. A divorce between the two is unreal and untrue to fact. Poetry should embody elements of actual experience, but set them in the light of the genuine ideal. In this we presume that the final truth of nature and man is the same, and this is the conclusion of sober philosophy. The earliest Upanishads of India with the latest systems of modern Critical Idealism assert that the principle which works

[1] Shakespeare.

in the human imagination as the ideal of man, and the end towards which nature moves by force of its immanent idea, are identical. What true poetry does is to shadow forth the identity of the whole, man and nature. Goethe's lines, as translated by Carlyle, bring out the true spirit of the poet :

> As all Nature's myriad changes still one changeless Power proclaim,
> So through Thought's wide kingdom ranges one vast Meaning, e'er the same :
> This is Truth—Eternal Reason—that in beauty takes its dress,
> And serene, through time and season, stands complete in righteousness.

The poets who lack this spirit are not of the right type, whatever their writings may achieve. The abiding judgment of man will put them down for counterfeit coin.

Rabindranath is of opinion that both realism and idealism in their extreme forms are wrong. To him realism, which would have art reproduce nature in all the coarse reality of its surface appearance, is as false a conception of poetry as idealism, which would not deign to walk the streets, but would fain fly in the medium of an ideal unrelated to fact. He adopts the true view, which is a higher union of the two, limiting both and fulfilling both. Art is concerned neither with the actual and the imperfect, nor with the ideal and the hazy, but with the natural transfigured by the ideal immanent in it. "I believe in an ideal life. I believe that, in a little flower, there is a living power hidden in beauty which is more potent than a Maxim gun. I believe that in the bird's notes Nature expresses herself with a force which is greater than that revealed in the deafening roar of the cannonade. I believe that there is an ideal hovering over the earth, —an ideal of that Paradise which is not the mere outcome of imagination, but the ultimate reality towards which all things are moving. I believe that this vision of Paradise is to be seen in the sunlight, and the green of the earth, in the flowing streams, in the beauty of springtime and the repose of a winter morning. Everywhere in this earth the spirit of Paradise is awake and sending forth its voice. . . ."[1] So deep is Rabindranath's love of nature that to him every aspect of nature becomes a symbol

[1] *Shantiniketan*, by W. W. Pearson; Epilogue by Rabindranath Tagore.

of beauty. He does not love nature for its own sake, but because he views it as an attribute of the divine; not for the abundance of joy that it brings into life, but for the intimations it gives of a higher spiritual life. To him even a blade of grass or an atom of dust brings a message from the unknown. To him every flower is a symbol of worship, every garland a gitanjali, every forest a temple, and every hill-top God's dwelling-place. The sound of the running water, the rustle of the leaves, and the song of the bird are so many hymns of praise to the great God. He has faith in the soul of the universe. He cannot be a great poet who has no faith in it. It is a philosophy of divine immanence that should be at the basis of true and great poetry. The East has faith in this universal soul. To the Indian poet this universal Presence is not a mere matter of philosophical speculation, but is as real as the sunlight or the earth under his feet.[1] To him "in Art the person in us is sending its answers to the Supreme Person, who reveals Himself to us in a world of endless beauty across the lightless world of

[1] *Personality*, p. 27.

facts."[1] The actual hides the ideal; the natural the spiritual; and what art does is to reveal the hidden spiritual ideal. The destiny of nature is to become spirit. The function of the artist or the poet is to exalt the natural towards its destined spiritual perfection. The poet releases the spirit imprisoned in matter. When the poet, oppressed by the idealism which fills his body and soul, touches matter it loses its materiality. What is common loses its commonness, what is earthy loses its earthiness, and what is finite and imperfect its finiteness and imperfection. The poet's mind, dominated by an overpowering sense of the spiritual, penetrates through the veil of their earthly covering into the life of things. The Greek view that there are certain objects which are beautiful and others ugly, and the artist has only to take note of them, loses its force. The Greek framed his images of gods from perfect human models which he looked upon as beautiful. But the Hindu does not care for the human models, but simply surrenders himself to the spontaneity of the spiritual vision. "The artist,"

[1] *Personality*, p. 38.

says Sukracharya, "should attain to the images of the gods by means of spiritual contemplation only. The spiritual vision is the best and truest standard for him. He should depend upon it, and not at all upon the visible objects perceived by external senses. . . . It is far better to present the figure of a god, though it is not beautiful, than to reproduce a remarkably handsome human figure."[1] To Rabindranath, as to Indian thought in general, beauty is subjective. Anything may be made the vehicle for it. Even the grotesque is not useless. "In Art, man reveals himself and not his objects."[2] We should have the spiritual harmony, and then the whole world will burst into music. Everything depends on us. "It is like our touch upon the harp-string: if it is too feeble, then we are merely aware of the touch, but if it is strong, then our touch comes back to us in tunes and our consciousness is intensified."[3] So the harp-string is neither the one nor the other. Everything depends on our touch, whether it is feeble or strong; in other words,

[1] See Havell's *Indian Sculpture and Painting*, pp. 54-55.
[2] *Personality*, p. 12. [3] *Ibid.* p. 15.

whether we are full of spiritual fire or not. Or we may put it the other way, and say that the soul with the fire in it is like some stringed instrument, and any object which strikes it produces sound. "The one effort of man's personality is to transform everything with which he has any true concern into the human. And art is like the spread of vegetation, to show how far man has reclaimed the desert for his own."[1] The things of the world are rescued from the flux of time and the relativity of space, and viewed under the light that never was on sea or land. To the eye of the genuine poet the spiritual aspects are as simple and natural and as real as the sea or the sunlight to the naked eye. In true poetry the real is idealised, and the ideal realised, and we have quite a genuine but a higher kind of real object. As Tennyson puts it, poetry is truer than fact. So the greatest poetry must embody an ideal vision or a true philosophy. Without this philosophic vision no great poetry can exist. Poetry may charm us by its wit, surprise us by its skill, thrill us by its richness, amuse us by its variety, lull

[1] *Personality*, p. 29.

us into sleep by its rhythm, and satisfy our craving for extraordinary incident; but let it lack the vision, it sinks to the level of verse and ceases to be poetry.

V

Poetry is creative while prose is narrative; poetry is an end in itself while prose is a means to an end. A genuine poet has the creative vision which makes beauty. The peace of the soul will work out in terms of visible beauty, and the poet by swift image and noble phrase puts forth his ideal. If the creation is present, it is poetry whether it is in verse or not. Rules of prosody are for the poet and not the poet for them. Rules are his servants and not his masters. Technique is only a means to an end. Those who observe technique and make rhyming lines without any creative idea or spiritual vision are versifiers and not poets. Their products are verses and not poems. Verses can be turned out with a certain number of feet, but not poetry, which requires the artistic vision and inspiration. Technique will not make for vitality. It may even be said that an art which follows rules is an art without beauty. It is like religion without faith, morality without heroism. There are people who imagine that it matters not what the poet says, provided he says it well. But this is to separate matter and form, which we cannot in justice do. To Rabindranath the vision and the form in which it is bodied forth are inseparable. The soul and the body are one; the outward is the expression of the inward.[1] "It is meritorious," writes Carlyle, "to insist on forms. Religion and all else naturally clothes itself in forms. All substances clothe themselves in forms; but there are suitable true forms, and then there are untrue, unsuitable. As the briefest definition one might say, Forms which grow round a substance, if we rightly understand that, will correspond to the real Nature and purport of it, will be true, good; forms which are consciously put round a substance, bad." Similarly S. T. Coleridge observes: "The form is mechanic when on any given material we impress a predetermined form, not necessarily arising out of the properties of the material—as

[1] *Personality*, p. 20.

when to a mass of wet clay we give whatever shape we wish it to retain when hardened. The organic form, on the other hand, is innate; it shapes as it develops itself from within, and the fulness of its development is one and the same with the perfection of its outward form. Such as the life is, such is the form."[1] Form and substance are of a piece; they are made for each other. As water makes its channel, so the substance creates its form. In poetry the spirit becomes incarnate and the body becomes instinct with spirit. The essential point is the creative vision, and if art should be the expression of it, it will do. Art should be the expression of life and should be informed by it. In the absence of the vision, poetry becomes merely an academic affectation or pedantic word-display. There are critics who think that Rabindranath is not a great poet because he disregards poetic form. But form is only the vehicle for the vision, the means for self-realisation. The end of art is not the realisation of form, but that of spirit. Art is more the expression of thought than the revelation of form. India never worshipped form for its own

[1] *Lectures.*

sake. Indian theory of art agrees with Hegel in thinking that "the outward shape by which the content is made perceptible is merely there for the sake of mind and spirit."[1] The artist tries to represent not the form but the ideal. He tries to materialise the idea, show us the subtle soul. The idolatry of form to be met with in the West is due to a confusion about the object of art. The aim of art is self-expression; and this it realises by the arts, sculpture and painting, music and poetry. Beauty happens to be the main element of this expression, and so it is thought that the production of beauty is the aim of art, "whereas beauty in art has been the mere instrument and not its complete and ultimate significance."[2] It is this conception of beauty as the end of art that makes some people imagine that manner is more important than matter. A poetic genius like Rabindranath need not be bound by forms. He is a law unto himself, makes his own rules and breaks through the ordinary conventions. Feeling that convention is the curse of poetry, realising that rhymes have a restricting effect on the free flight of the

[1] *Aesthetics*, i. 91. [2] *Personality*, p. 19.

poetic spirit, Rabindranath employs the rhythmical prose which is turned to such good account in *The Song of Solomon* and Whitman's *Leaves of Grass*. How well the soul of Rabindranath's poetry has shaped its body may be seen by taking any of his poems at random. We have music and melody in his poems as well as sweetness and light. What, after all, is the good of poetry where the freedom of spirit is lost in the desert sands of dead forms? It does not come into the group of poetry at all, unless the breath of life blows over the desert sands and makes them blossom into fruits and flowers.

VI

If poetry is so closely related to philosophy, to what is their traditional opposition due? A false idea of philosophy is responsible for it. A philosopher is supposed to be one who merely feeds his intellect at the expense of the whole man. His heart and moral nature are left starving. We have a representative of this type in the Pundit of *The Cycle of Spring*, who, while talking glibly of renunciation and worldly wisdom, is most selfish, and wants to dole out by bits his learning to the king in "exchange for the rich province of Kanchanpur," while the poet with true detachment "never accepts reward" for preaching love and charity.[1] The Pundit, who, like "the newer people of the modern age," is "more eager to amass than to realise,"[2] cannot see deeper than the surfaces of things, and his outlook is sordid, materialist, and utilitarian. To him—

> If bamboos were made only into flutes,
> They would droop and die with very shame.
> They hold their heads high in the sky,
> Because they are variously useful.[3]

He is sorry that the "numerous stars in the midnight sky which hang in the air for no purpose," do not come down to earth for street lighting, and thus help the ratepayer.[4] The Pundit has before him the ideal of usefulness, while the poet has that of enjoyment. One bows down before machinery, while the other worships personality. One has the practical, worldly, business point of view, while the other has the childlike, unworldly point of view. The poet is for dreams and not business. To him who is an infant in worldly affairs things appear in their spiritual significance. It is

[1] P. 22. [2] *Ibid.* p. 32. [3] *Ibid.* p. 47. [4] *Ibid.* p. 49.

clear that mere intellect will not make a great poet any more than an honest trader or a good governor. The philosophical ideal, we have already seen, cannot be reached by intellectual categories. To catch sight of the philosophical ideal we require meditation and mystic insight. Intellect revelling in distinctions and opposites can give us, in the words of Bradley, an unearthly ballet of bloodless categories which is no substitute for the concrete riches of life. For the synthetic vision and the reconciling view we have to transcend intellect by means of intuition. "Full many an hour have I spent in the strife of the good and the evil, but now it is the pleasure of my playmate of the empty days to draw my heart on to him."[1] An intellectualist plays with words, concepts, and categories, but misses the truth and reality. Mysticism is the key which would open the door to the shrine where the "invisible king" is. "The dust of the dead words cling to thee, wash thy soul with silence."[2] So if the term Philosopher is taken in the sense of an intellectual metaphysician paying homage to the logical intellect and not an intuitive seer, then

[1] *Gitanjali*, 89.

[2] *Stray Birds*, 147.

poetry has nothing to do with philosophy. In the story of "The Victory," Rabindranath gives us a description of the genuine poet as distinguished from the counterfeit. The intellectual poet Pundarik is contrasted with the true poet Shekhar, the poet of King Nārāyan. The king received Pundarik with honour and said, "Poet, I offer you welcome." Pundarik proudly replied, "Sire, I ask for war." But "Shekhar, the court poet of the king, did not know how the battle of the muse was to be waged."[1] Here is the contrast between the arrogance of the word-builder and the humility of the true poet. "With a trembling heart Shekhar entered the arena in the morning. . . . With his head held high and chest expanded, he (Pundarik) began in his thundering voice to recite the praise of King Nārāyan. . . . The skill with which he gave varied meanings to the name Nārāyan, and wove each letter of it through the web of his verses in all manner of combinations, took away the breath of his amazed hearers." Such is the way the world judges poets. The effect of the performance on the audience was one of astonishment

[1] *Hungry Stones*, p. 32.

at the intellectual profundity of the phrase-maker and the versifier. But Shekhar produced just the opposite effect. When he began he was full of feeling ready to burst out. "His face was pale, his bashfulness was almost that of a woman, his slight youthful figure, delicate in its outline, seemed like a tensely strung *vina* ready to break out in music at the least touch." And when Shekhar finished what was the effect? "Tears filled the eyes of the hearers, and the stone walls shook with cries of victory." Such is the effect of true art. When true music is heard, rafters ring, serpents sing, the very stones melt, and the whole world dances, as some Indian poets would have it. Pundarik stands for stupendous learning, and in the conceit of his knowledge he asks: "What is there superior to words?" To him "the Word was in the beginning, and the Word was God." But what did Shekhar prove? "Next day Shekhar began his song. It was of that day when the pipings of love's flute startled for the first time the hushed air of the *vrinda* forest. The shepherd women did not know who was the player or whence came the music. Sometimes it seemed to come from the heart of the south wind, and sometimes from the straying clouds of the hill-tops. It came with a message of tryst from the land of the sunrise, and it floated from the verge of sunset with its sigh of sorrow. The stars seemed to be the stops of the instrument that flooded the dreams of the night with melody. The music seemed, to burst all at once from all sides, from fields and groves, from the shady lanes and lonely roads, from the melting blue of the sky, from the shimmering green of the grass. They neither knew its meaning nor could they find words to give utterance to the desire of their hearts. Tears filled their eyes, and their life seemed to long for a death that would be its consummation." The true poet forgets himself in his poetry. "Shekhar forgot his audience, forgot the trial of his strength with a rival. He stood alone amid his thoughts that rustled and quivered round him like leaves in a summer breeze, and sang the Song of the Flute." He attains that exaltation and freedom where the individual becomes free from self-consciousness. The trappings of the world fall away and he sees things as they are, and sings his inspired poetry. He feels the whole world to be a harmony and all nature music. He is not a man of words but full of feeling. When Shekhar took his seat "his hearers trembled with the sadness of an indefinable delight, immense and vague, and they forgot to applaud him." In other words, they were filled with freedom and careless joy. Pundarik challenged his rival to define who was the lover and who was the beloved, and "then he began to analyse the roots of those names.[1] Each letter of those names he divided from its fellow, and then pursued them with a relentless logic till they fell to the dust in confusion, to be caught up again and restored to a meaning never before imagined by the subtlest of word-mongers." Who were the men to appreciate this wonderful gymnastics? "The pundits were in ecstasy." A thin, stiff, and straight vision was what the intellectualist conjured up. "The atmosphere was completely cleared of all illusion of music, and the vision of the world around seemed to be changed from its freshness of tender green to the solidity of a high road levelled and made hard with crushed

[1] Radha and Krishna.

stones." But the king declared that Pundarik had the victory. Shekhar returned home and threw his writings into the fire, for they were "mere words and childish rhymes." At night "he spread upon his bed the white flowers that he loved, the jasmines, and opened wide his windows," and drank a poisonous juice. Then Ajita appeared on the scene, "and it seemed to him that the image made of a shadow that he had ever kept throned in the secret shrine of his heart had come into the outer world in his last moments to gaze upon his face." "The princess whispered into his ear: 'The king has not done you justice. It was you who won at the combat, my poet, and I have come to crown you with the crown of victory.'" As he was singing, joy, the secret of the universe, was being laid bare. Pundarik beats down his hearers by mere words, dumbfounds them by his intellectual subtleties, and makes them believe that giving names to things and calling relations categories is to explain them. In his arrogance he feels that the secret of the universe is to be found in his waistcoat pocket. He thinks that he has a key which would unlock the doors of all problems in heaven and earth, and a good many in neither. Everything from the stars of heaven to the shells of earth had a fixed place in his scheme of the universe. But the pity of it is that intellectual legerdemain does not constitute truth and poetry. Poetry is a cry of the spirit and it has nothing to do with pretences born and bred of books, as these are useless to the spirit. The people along with the king who applauded him did so because they were "deluded into the certainty that they had witnessed, that day, the last shred of the curtains of Truth torn to pieces by a prodigy of intellect. But they forgot to ask if there was any truth behind it after all."[1] Victory was beaming from the breast of Pundarik and found response in the king's heart. And the people caught the suggestion from the king and were hypnotised into admiration of Pundarik. They neither considered nor questioned, but, carried away by the tide, threw their hats up, cheered him, and jumped for joy. No wonder Pundarik triumphed. Such is the way reputations are built in this world. Thus Rabindranath points out that intellectual

[1] *Hungry Stones*, chap. ii.

poetry is a contradiction in terms. So if by philosopher we mean an intellectual juggler, then philosophy has nothing to do with poetry. But if by philosopher we mean the intuitive seer who has risen above his small self, a man who has attained true freedom of consciousness, then he is one with the poet who hears the whispers of the soul and gives voice to them. Such were the ancient Rishis who broke away from the fetters and revealed their souls in the Upanishads. And such is Rabindranath.

It is often urged that poetry and philosophy are opposed because poetry deals with life, becoming, movement, while philosophy deals with stillness, rest, and immutability. Philosophy is represented as being thin, lifeless, and unsubstantial, while poetry is regarded as rich, warm, and glowing. But we have seen that this description of philosophy is unjust and one-sided. While a few systems conclude that being alone is real and not becoming, the attempt of philosophy is to gather in a whole both being and becoming. Modern systems of concrete idealism present us with such reconciling wholes. Neither philosophy nor poetry deals with things as they appear, but concerns itself with things as they really are. Both poetry and philosophy are criticisms of life at first sight or interpretations thereof. Both protest against "the sloth which takes things as they are, and the poorness of spirit which is satisfied with first appearances." And so this charge that philosophy deals with abstractions while poetry deals with life is unfounded.

VII

The poet worships God as the spirit of beauty, while the philosopher pays his homage to God as the ideal of truth. Philosophy is the temple of truth, while poetry is the shrine of beauty. The two are not opposed, as truth is beauty and beauty truth. Reality is absolute, though there are many ways of realising it. Philosophy tells us how a synoptic vision which binds together all terms and relations in a concrete spiritual whole is the Real. Poetry individualises this vision of philosophy. Rabindranath, as is obvious from the chapters dealing with his philosophy, is a reflective thinker, but in him reason and reflection are subordinated to imagination and emotion. His philosophical views are caught up in his spiritual vision and held captive in his poetic creations. The spirit of his poetry is the spirit of his life. The abstract and intellectual categories become suffused with the glow and warmth of things seen and realised. The example of Rabindranath Tagore, if examples were needed, would give the lie direct to the cry, which even the street urchin of the present day raises, that mysticism is incompatible with good poetry. To these critics it matters little if Dante and Goethe and many of the classical poets of religious Asia held the opposite view, and asserted and practised the doctrine that all true poetry is mystic. The authors of the Upanishads were poet-philosophers. Most of the great Persian poets were Sufi or mystic philosophers, who had for their aim the attainment of a state of spiritual perfection where the soul will be absorbed in holy contemplation to the exclusion of the pleasures of the world. Eternity is in the looks and eyes of these poets. Philosophy and religion are counted among the creative forces which moulded Asiatic art and poetry. Mr. Havell observes: "Indian art is not concerned with the conscious striving after beauty as a thing worthy to be sought after for its own sake; its main endeavour is always directed towards the realisation of an idea, reaching through the finite to the infinite, convinced always that, through the constant effort to express the spiritual origin of earthly beauty, the human mind will take in more and more of the perfect beauty of divinity."[1] The same point is thus described by Mr. Laurence Binyon: "Not the glory of the naked human form, to Western art the noblest and most expressive of symbols; not the proud and conscious assertion of human personality; but, instead of these, all thoughts that lead us out from ourselves into the universal life, hints of the infinite, whispers from secret sources,—mountains, waters, mists, flowering trees, whatever tells of powers and presences mightier than ourselves; these are the themes dwelt upon, cherished and preferred."[2] It is the aim of Indian art to relate the seen and the unseen, the material and the spiritual, through imagination. The "building of man's true world . . . is

[1] *Ideals of Indian Art*, p. 32.
[2] *Painting in the Far East*, p. 22.

the function of Art. Man is true, where he feels his infinity, where he is divine, and the divine is the creator in him."[1] Browning, speaking of the subjective poet, observes that he "is impelled to embody the thing he perceives, not so much with reference to the many below, as to the one above him . . . not what man sees, but what God sees—it is toward these that he struggles." We cannot therefore say that because Rabindranath's poetry is mystic it is not good poetry. It is undoubtedly mystic, and on that account he should hold a permanent place in the firmament of world-poets.

VIII

While both philosophy and poetry aim at the same end, their starting-points are different. They approach reality from different angles. While philosophy aims at grasping the synthesis which gathers together all aspects of the universe, poetry aims at catching the vision which sees the things of beauty of the world as a whole. Philosophy is an attempt to conceive the world as a whole by means of thought. It aims at a theory of the universe; and if this

[1] *Personality*, p. 31.

theory is held with a certain intensity and depth of feeling, if it captures the whole consciousness instead of being merely intellectually assented to, then the philosophic vision becomes creative and poetic. Thought suffused with feeling and the other elements of consciousness becomes exalted into contemplation. The soul in this mood acquires imaginative vision with its spontaneity and creativity. It is then called mystic. But so long as the theory remains a mere intellectual creed, the difference between philosophy and poetry is kept up. The philosopher has his hand firm on the distinctions which are reconciled in the thought synthesis, and his reconciliation remains abstract and conceptual. The poet does not reason, but intuits. He does not make guesses at truth, but feels the truth as deeply real, and fierce with meaning. He lives life, and distils his doctrines from life. The living unity of life is given in poetry in all its immediacy and concreteness, while it is only argued about in philosophical dissertations. The hard distinctions of philosophy melt into a sweet harmony in the flow of poetry. But the true philosopher with the true poet follows the intuitive method.

Both are characterised by self-forgetfulness and spontaneity. The vision creative and the poetic impulse burst out like a volcanic force. Plato's description of the poet as one who is bereft of reason but filled with divinity, holds good of the philosopher also. Our conclusion is, that a poet is nothing if he is not a philosopher. A true poet will be a philosopher, and a true philosopher a poet.

IX

Philosophy tells us that the world is rational; poetry tells us that it is beautiful. Philosophy reconciles the world to our reason; poetry to our feelings. Disorder and irrationality, philosophy cannot tolerate; ugliness and disgust with nature and society, poetry cannot accept. The greatest tragedies are tragic only at first sight; the poet finds in them a world of goodness. He shows us how sorrow "is not sorrow but delight."[1] The world is after all lovable. Poetry attunes our soul to the world and makes us feel that the world is a place worth living in. This he does, not by concepts and arguments, but by music and fancy. Poetry pleases

[1] Wordsworth.

by an immediate appeal to imagination, and convinces not the intellect but the soul. The vision which the philosopher sees, the poet recreates. He realises it in his work. In poetry, philosophy lives. It puts on flesh and blood. It gives us not the philosophic idea, but the idea as lived or the life of the idea. For the spread of philosophy and true knowledge, nothing is so good a medium as poetry. It spreads truth more quietly. Truth slides into the mind unconsciously, effortlessly, easily. Wordsworth says: "That which comes from the heart goes to the heart." Poetry is not intended to be a statement of truth, but only an expression of experience. It expresses what is held within the heart. By flooding the soul with emotions, by steeping the spirit in a bath of joy or delight, poetry puts the reader *en rapport* with the mind of the poet, induces him to sympathise with his temper, and breathe the atmosphere which floats before his eyes, and in which the poet lives, moves, and has his being. Poetry is a flower to be smelt, a sweet to be tasted or "drunk in every limb," [1] and not taught. It does not cram the mind with

[1] Hegel.

facts and theories, but gives it a direction. It does not teach, but touches the heart, warms the emotions, and moulds the whole mind. As an instrument of propagating knowledge, it is better than philosophy; for while a philosophic conclusion may commend itself to the intellect, it may quite possibly be regarded as incapable of satisfying the other sides of human life, though a true philosophic conclusion would satisfy not merely the intellect, but life as a whole. Philosophy may satisfy man the knower, but he is "not fully himself."[1] In poetry we need have no such fear; for the appeal is to the whole personality of man. The "world, which takes its form in the mould of man's perception, still remains only as the partial world of his senses and mind. It is like a guest and not like a kinsman. It becomes completely our own when it comes within the range of our emotions."[2] Poetry "brings to us ideas, vitalised by feelings, ready to be made into the life-stuff of our nature."[3] We have the assurance that the poet has lived what he is giving voice to, for he speaks straight out of life. "Consciously or unconsciously,

[1] *Personality*, p. 13. [2] *Ibid.* p. 14. [3] *Ibid.* p. 15.

I may have done many things that were untrue, but I have never uttered anything false in my poetry,—that is the sanctuary where the deepest truths of my life emerge."[1] The work of the poet bears the impress of his life and individuality, and what is a part of one man's life can surely enter others' lives. The poet speaks as man to other men. Poetry appeals to the mind as a whole, for it is the expression of mind's free and unrestrained work. Besides, all true poetry forces acceptance of the poet's message, as he expresses it with such a passion and feeling, force and fulness, that to read it is to be convinced of it. The appeal of the artist compels into acquiescence those who cannot grasp the reasoning of philosophy. If the truth of the world cannot be hammered into a man's head by the engines of argument and proof, the beauty of the poet's verse may yet win a way to the heart, and succeed where reasoning has failed. In the presence of its fancy and fragrance, music and sound, man feels helpless and his critical faculty sinks into silence. Poetry rouses the imagination and lets logic slumber and reason

[1] Rabindranath Tagore, Letters, *Modern Review*, July 1917.

rest. The soul thinks, feels, and enjoys with the poet. Poetry attunes the soul to the life of truth, and the reader sees truth with the eye of the mind, and hears it with the ears of the soul. By its music and melody, poetry induces consent, disarms criticism, and overpowers the soul. It has in it the power to coerce, or rather charm, the unwilling mind into homage. We do not ask for proof in poetry, for poetry is its own proof, "truth is its own testimony." If Rabindranath has touched Indian hearts, it is because he is first and foremost a poet and not a philosopher. But in all his works he has in view the great ideal of ancient Hindu art, viz. "to make the central ideas of Hindu religion and philosophy intelligible to all Hinduism, to satisfy the unlettered but not unlearned Hindu peasant as well as the intellectual Brahmin."[1] The highly abstruse notions of Hindu philosophy and religion are set free in his songs from their academic isolation and become a part of the common life of men. Rabindranath is following the tradition of the great Indian Rishis who spoke what they felt in the lyric songs

[1] Havell, *The Ideals of Indian Art*, Introduction xviii.

of the Upanishads and their other creations. The devotional and poetic literature of India is embodied in poetry and music. By means of the epic poetry of India, the *Ramayana* and the *Mahabharata*, the priest and the peasant, the prince and the workman have become acquainted with the essentials of Hindu religion and philosophy, thought out by the sages of India. Art has penetrated so deeply into the national life of India that the Indian peasant-folk, though illiterate in the sense of unlettered, can challenge comparison in point of culture with their corresponding classes anywhere in the world. Mr. Yeats observes in his Introduction to the *Gitanjali*: "A tradition, where poetry and religion are the same thing, has passed through the centuries, gathering from learned and unlearned metaphor and emotion, and carried back again to the multitude the thought of the scholar and the noble."[1] By making truth live in forms of beauty the poet forces his ideas into the life of man. Truth enters into man's nature through the gate of emotion. While it is true that poetry is not didactic and does not teach, still it thrills

[1] Page xiv.

the reality and burns its ideas into the emotional nature of man. True to the saying of Plutarch, that poetry should initiate us into philosophy, Rabindranath's writings are waking many to the possibilities of spiritual life. His songs have become national songs, replete with words that breathe and thoughts that burn. His words please the ear, his ideas sink into the heart. His poetry is at the same time a light that fills the mind, a song that stirs the blood, and a hymn that moves the heart. The voice of Rabindranath, vibrating with the passion of genius, and glorifying all his race, instils into the sinking heart of India faith in herself, faith in her future, and faith in the world.

CHAPTER IV

THE MESSAGE OF RABINDRANATH TAGORE TO INDIA

Here the singer for his art
  Not all in vain may plead,
The song that moves a nation's heart
  Is in itself a deed.

TENNYSON.

The old Arab tribes would gather in liveliest gaudeamus, and sing, and kindle bonfires, and wreathe crowns of honour, and solemnly thank the gods that in their tribe, too, a poet had shown himself. As, indeed, they well might; for what usefuller, I say not nobler and heavenlier thing, could the gods, doing their very kindest, send to any tribe or nation, in any time or circumstance.—CARLYLE.

I

THERE are men rare in any age, but unique in our age, to whom it is given to shape the mind of their country to an extent that cannot be rightly estimated in their own lifetime. Rabindranath Tagore is such a man, and the debt which modern India owes to him, we cannot pretend to measure. His teaching is penetrating the most out-of-the way and distant corners of India; the amount of moral regeneration and social uplift which his work will accomplish, it is quite impossible to say now. To the people of India, he is a prophet with a message. In the true sense of the word he is a national poet. India fills his heart as nothing else does. He sees what India wants, and tells us what exactly it is. He sees the inward agonising of the Indian soul, understands the passions and doubts surging in her mind, wishes to deliver her from the travail through which she is passing, and give her peace of soul. He pours forth in his supreme song the dreams and aspirations which are moving the mind of India. The joys and sorrows, the hopes and fears, the doubts and beliefs of the Indian life are captured in his books. Adapting Johnson, we might say that the work of Rabindranath abounds in sentiments to which every Indian bosom returns an echo. He gives voice to the doubts which are darkening the once glorious faith of India. It is the sign that God has not lost all hope of India that Rabindranath is born in this age. He is born at a time when there is a seething of religious beliefs and a lawless raging of social forces, the like of which has probably not been seen before. The poet of India that he is, he expresses and corrects the aspirations of the Indian community. He is the signpost warning India, which is at the parting of the ways, to pursue the path of spirit and relinquish that of matter. Deep down amidst the surging doubts, the foundations of a stronger faith in God and India's destiny are being slowly laid by the poet's work.

One of the rarest spirits that ever steered humanity, he is not without his message to the world. His message is most significant for us from the point of view of pure humanity. His writings are not narrowly national but are touched with a wider spirit. In him the voice of India speaks not only to Indians but to the world at large. To the British Empire he has a special charge, which he does not hide. The world in its present crisis appeals to him, and he has a mission to it. Dr. Sunderland, in the course of a contribution to the *Christian Register*, well observes: "No land in the world has ever produced profounder thinkers on all the problems of religion and life than the India of the past. The India of to-day has no wiser, kinder, more broad-minded, or greater teacher than Mr. Tagore, none more eager to receive from us whatever of value we have to give, or better able to impart to us the best wisdom of his own historic land." Rabindranath interprets this ancient wisdom of India to the world, and as transfigured by his poetry and music, as revised and brought up to date by his brilliant mind and culture, it has the power to satisfy the hunger of the spirit. The world respects him not merely for his richly endowed personality and many-sided nature, which come out in his beautiful poetry, but also for the spiritual message of his writings. He points to the plague spot of modern civilisation, which hurries along the highroad to the golden fountain and seeks by conquest to gain the whole world—no matter if in so doing it loses the soul.

II

The greatest of all problems which confront the patriot-reformer of India, who proposes to shatter the sorry scheme of things entire and remould it nearer to heart's desire, is the religious future of the country. The religious situation will have to be dealt with in a manner that would guarantee the spiritual progress of the country, and do justice to the bewildering variety of faiths and creeds, indigenous and foreign, which flourish in the land. Rabindranath dreams of and pictures to us a vision of India, purged of its superstitions and worshipping the One God, each in its own way, without quarrel or misunderstanding. In religion he stands for a passionate devotion to God. His is not the way of intellectual comprehension, but that of intuitive grasp. While the externals of worship divide, the deeper core of religious experience is essentially the same. The Sufi mystic, the Christian divine, and the Hindu Rishi agree in regarding creation as the manifestation of the eternal beauty of God; man, His emanation and perfection, becoming one with God. The philosophy of Rabindranath is an absolute idealism of the concrete type. His supreme spirit is not an abstract entity residing at a safe distance from the world, but is the concrete dynamic life at the centre of things, giving rise to the roar of the wind and the surge of the sea. It is the final truth of the cosmic dance of life and death. Rabindranath's is a wholeness of vision, which cannot tolerate absolute divisions between body and mind, matter and life, individual and society, community and nation, and empire and the world. Mystic experience the world over has this philosophy underlying it. Rabindranath's religious message is simple: Stick to religion, let religions go. Happiness is for those who realise this oneness and wholeness of spirit. It is for those who respond to the call of the divine in them.[1] To realise this goal, it is not necessary that the traditional paths should be followed; for the path of devotion is trackless.[2] Rabindranath gives us a pure religion, which is substantially the same in all ages and all climates, in which the purified spirit of man can find its congenial home. His religion is not hampered by any

[1] *Fruit-Gathering*, VII. [2] See *Ibid.* VI., XIV., XVI.

man-made formulas, or church ordinances which act as barriers. "When religion has to make way for religious organisation it is like the river being dominated by its sand-bed; the current stagnates and its aspects become desert-like."[1] Being free and pure, it finds its spiritual kin in all faiths and creeds. All types of souls can find genuine spiritual satisfaction in it. He sees fundamental unity in diversity, and so his religion appeals to all. In the Bolpur school there are Brahmos, Christians, and Hindus. The diversity of religious beliefs presents absolutely no difficulty, as nobody deals with dogmas of sectarianism. The poet insists on the worship of the one invisible God—it does not matter by what means. He knows that God fulfils Himself in many ways. His article on "The Appeal of Christ to India"[2] well brings out how near to the religion of Christ his religion is. He there asks: "Who else has glorified man in every way as he has done?" It is his hope that the world-religions which have met on the soil of India will cease to conflict with one

[1] *Modern Review*, September 1917, p. 335.
[2] *The Quest*, April 1916.

another, and reach a reconciliation. "Hindus, Buddhists, Muslims, and Christians will not fight each other on the soil of India; they will here seek and attain to a synthesis. That synthesis will not be un-Hindu, it will be peculiarly Hindu. Whatever its external features may be, the resultant harmony will be Indian in spirit."[1] Rabindranath works for the rebuilding of India, not on any narrow basis of creed, province, or language, but on the broad basis of India and her spiritual vision of universal love. Indians should work for the regeneration of India because they are all Indians, children of the same soil, descendants of the long line of Indian saints. The Hindu as well as the Muslim finds India to be the home of his noble ancestors; her earth contains the dust of his saints; she is his seat of righteousness and religion; in her progress lies his hope.

It is Rabindranath's sincere conviction that the Hindu religion can stand against the onslaught of Western civilisation, religion, and culture, on condition that it rids itself of its dogmatism and superstition. The Aryan faith,

[1] *Modern Review*, June 1913.

in its unsullied purity, can give unity to the chaotic channels pouring in floods into India from Western sources. But they will overwhelm the Indian faith, if it does not in the meantime look about itself, and with an unsparing hand cut off the weedy outgrowths. We must free ourselves from all the exhausted traditions, spent forces, and obsolete watchwords which still possess us. A spiritual religion like that of Rabindranath Tagore, which has for its ideal a right heart and a saintly character, which has for its principle love of God and service of man, can make no truce with idle rites and ceremonies, blind dogmas and superstitions, snobbery and pharisaism, orthodoxy of a priestly caste, pride and prejudice of position and authority, selfishness of classes and exclusiveness of nations. The soul of India has to be delivered from these besetting sins, and people like Rabindranath Tagore help in the process.

III

Among the evils which are poisoning the very springs of national life, the first and foremost is the caste system. Rabindranath is not oblivious to the purposes which it served, to the value of the principles on which it was framed. When the Aryans first came to India they had to encounter the previous inhabitants of the country. As the Aryans were dominated by the spiritual impulse, they did not adopt the lazy device of either extirpating the native peoples or reducing them to slavery, but organised a social system based on the recognition of spiritual unity as well as racial differences. The caste system when instituted was a social unity in which the different peoples could live together in mutual harmony while enjoying the freedom to maintain their differences. The social organisation of India was based on the principle of reconciliation and not discord. "It is not the case in Europe that all classes do their respective, legitimate functions, and thus try by their collective efforts to maintain the social organisation; on the contrary, they are mutually antagonistic: every class is always on the alert to prevent others from growing stronger. Thus the social harmony is destroyed. . . . India has tried to reconcile things that are mutually alien to each other. . . . She set limits to and fenced off all the rival conflicting forces of society, and thus made the social organism one, and capable of doing its complex functions."[1] About the class of Brahmins, it is his opinion that every good society should have a section corresponding to it. In the Indian social organisation, which is a work of art, the Brahmins are at the top, and are the recognised leaders of society. Though India passed through several vicissitudes in her political fortunes, the society has not been much shaken, as her ideals and traditions were long preserved by this class. The Brahmins are the trustees of tradition and the conservers of the religious spirit. The Brahmins, according to the ideal, count poverty a privilege, consider learning their calling, and pursue the ideals of spirit with self-sacrifice and in a disinterested manner. Scorn of wealth and the pursuit of spirituality, reckless of praise or blame, are their characteristic features. Division of labour is now recognised to be a valid principle not only in economics but in other matters also, social organisation included. If we cannot make our clothes or our shoes for ourselves, if specially

[1] *Modern Review*, December 1910.

trained men can do these things much better than we can for ourselves, why should we not have a class set apart for artistic production and spiritual discovery? Members of this class are to discover and bring home to the community the joy of art and spiritual beauty. Automatically this class happens to be considered higher than the others, for while the tradesman and the merchant contribute to the physical needs, the members of this class are the purveyors of spiritual health and joy to the community. These are the leaders of society, regulating the things in which the community ought to take pleasure, exerting great moral influence on them. Those who are in the thick of the strife of the world have not the time to think of the welfare of the whole community, or to contemplate the higher things of life. But this is not to defend the present degraded and degenerated Brahmin class. These have done, besides much good, much evil in the name of God. As they have lost their old self-sacrifice and spirituality they have no claim to the respect and regard of the other classes. It is because they drilled the other classes into submission, and decreed their inferiority, that they fell in esteem and prestige. They crippled the minds of the Sudras, and to-day the insult has come back—their minds are being crippled. "When the Sudra joined his palms in submission to the brahmanical decree of inferiority, on that very day was dug the pit for the fall of the Brahmins."[1] They want the powers and prestige of the old Brahmin class, but they do not possess their ideals and spiritual strength which would win respect. Hence the bathos. But there is no question that the hierarchy of values incorporated in the caste system of India is right. The highest place is given to the philosopher who finds his lifework in search for truth, artistic creation, and moral endeavour. While the work of the philosopher is the recognised aim of society, the political stability and economic basis of it are also secured. Preserving peace and political order is the function of the warrior community. Classes for trading and agricultural interests are also included. It is an aristocratic organisation, where every function has a definite value assigned to it, and the scale of values depends not upon the amount of wealth, but on the

[1] *Modern Review*, September 1917, p. 337

development of the soul. Rise in the social scale is determined not by increase in wealth, but by ascent of spirit. We ought not to abandon this judgment of values. The Western civilisation, which is a civilisation of the rich, measures status by bank balances. With such a material aim and basis, selfishness and competition increase. But the Indian system has no ideas of propertied respectability. The caste system aims at universal brotherhood and love. Freedom is its basis and freedom its end. Man is looked upon as an end in himself, and not a mere creature of the moment, whom we can use for our purposes and then throw off. He is an eternal being whose purpose and destiny are to express his free spirit in actions of the world. The modern class system of the West is material in its outlook, while the caste system is spiritual. Realising that the material display of modern life conceals within it flimsiness of faith, and cannot satisfy the deeper needs of man, we have to take a lesson from the caste system, and build a spiritual civilisation on love and brotherhood, freedom and fellowship. This does not mean that we are holding a brief for the caste system as it prevails in India at the present day. We are aware that we have come to a time when that institution requires modification. The rigid and exclusive caste system has served its purpose and must vanish. Rabindranath writes: "It has largely contributed to the freedom from narrowness and intolerance which distinguishes the Hindu religion, and has enabled races with widely different cultures and even antagonistic social and religious usages and ideals to settle down peaceably side by side. . . . But this very absence of struggle, developing into a ready acquiescence in any position assigned by the social system, has crushed individual manhood, and has accustomed us for centuries not only to submit to every form of domination, but sometimes actually to venerate the power that holds us down. . . . The regeneration of the Indian people, to my mind, directly and perhaps solely depends upon the removal of this condition."[1] The institution of caste served a purpose till not long ago, but to-day it is a positive hindrance to the spiritual faith within and progress outside. The caste system

[1] *Modern Review*, August 1910 and February 1911.

failed to recognise the flow of life, the mobility of mind, and the mutability of characteristics. It failed to realise "that in human beings differences are not like the physical barriers of mountains, fixed for ever,—they are fluid with life's flow, they are changing their courses and their shapes and volume." The soul of the caste system has departed, and what India is now worshipping with awe and veneration is a dead corpse. The vast social mechanism created by man is now crushing the soul. Independent thinking and individuality are suppressed. The individual is caught in the wheels of the machine, and the machine will have to give up its nature, for man to regain life and soul. If like the child Amal in the *Post Office* we cripple our minds and narrow our freedom by confining it to our closed prisons and taking the directions of our traditional doctors, the Shastras, we shall not recover from our illusions. As the child longs to be out, mind craves for freedom. But we have to break open the gates and pull down the walls of our closed house, for the air and light of God to pour in and enlighten us.

Rabindranath does not view the social

problems of the time from the narrow economic or utilitarian point of view. He brings his spiritual vision to bear on the social problems, and lifts them up to a higher idealist plane. His attitude to them is determined, not by the accident of birth, habit, or training, but by the spiritual vision, the one central principle to which he devotes his whole life. The present social unrest would be at an end if people adopted the right attitude to life, and developed reverence for the divine in man. The materialist view of life makes us afraid of poverty, and in nations of spiritual vision, poverty is not the cause of social discontent. India is very poor, but centuries of spiritual discipline have given the Indian peoples so much restraint and self-suppression that though the problem of poverty is most intense in India, social unrest and struggle are greater in the West. When a great famine invades the country, or death-dealing plague stalks through the land, the Indian people submit to it in meek resignation. In suffering and distress they beg and pray, mope and pine, and, at worst, weep and die in silence, handing over their souls to God. We do not hear of strikes and riots, breaking windows and throwing bombs, mass movements and demonstrations of starving women and children. Their calm acceptance of pain and silent submission to suffering are the wonder of the world. Their patience of spirit dimly suggests the Cross of Calvary, the immortal reproach of divine virtue and wisdom against the blows of evil and circumstance. A materialist view of life is the root cause ot social discontent, and the remedy for the social unrest is a spiritual one. Professor L. P. Jacks observes: "It is not the poorest nations which reveal the maximum of social discontent. It is the richest. And the prime cause does not lie in the sense of inequality between individuals who have more and individuals who have less: that no doubt is a cause, but secondary. The root evil is that a community which makes wealth its object, and pursues it on the terms laid down by the economic machine, is living under conditions which satisfy nobody and against which all men are by the higher human nature born rebels."[1] The troubles of the Western nations are due to the predominance of the

[1] *International Crisis*, p. 99.

economic motive. Nations have for their ideal economic efficiency. The greatest output is the prime consideration. Man becomes but a cogwheel in the great machine. At the altar of this machine, human victims are sacrificed. Men, women, and children, and values of spirit are given the go-by. At the present day we find that the people are highly sensitive to all this loss, but with the best will in the world they are not able to get rid of the troubles of industrialism. It is because they consider them economic problems and devise economic remedies. But so long as we are moving within the charmed circle of economics, we cannot cure these ills. In condemning them as evils, it is not our economic side that asserts itself, but our human nature. We then occupy a higher standpoint; for the economic policy requires them and so must justify them. The solution lies in the steadfast occupancy of the higher, human, or spiritual point of view. India has had this spiritual ideal, and unless she preserves it there is no chance for her. India cannot regain her former prestige and glory by merely tinkering here and there with the social system, or getting a few more seats on the councils, or by the substitution of manufactures for cottage industries. If India becomes free in soul and preserves her spiritual individuality, then all other things shall be added unto her. "Then in India, province will join province, race will join race, knowledge will be linked with knowledge, endeavour with endeavour: then the present chapter of Indian history will end, and she will emerge in the larger history of the world."[1]

Educated Indians of the present day are not quite in sympathy with Rabindranath's ideal of preserving the national identity of India, and feel that India's salvation lies in the imitation of the West. That way lies madness. In their eagerness to save their skins, they forget it will ultimately be more profitable to save their souls. If the educated classes do not realise it, it is only the sign of how far the disease has gone, and the case is so much the worse. It is impossible to believe, unless one acquainted with the inspiration of ancient India sees for oneself, the extent to which modern India has succumbed, body and soul, to the materialist influence. These Indians pride themselves that

[1] *The Future of India.*

they are practical. What a price it costs to be practical to-day! Their soul is the price they pay. There is no use in acquiring the externals and the outward forms of a political civilisation and losing the soul. Imitation, according to Rabindranath Tagore, is "like dressing our skeleton with another man's skin, giving rise to eternal feuds between the skin and the bones at every movement."[1] If the political salvation of India is to be attained at the expense of her soul, we had better preserve the soul and lose the earthly kingdom. India then will vindicate spirit. And if she is doomed to disappear, then will she die with dignity, with the colours of spirit flying. "But let us stand firm and suffer with strength for the True, for the Good, for the Eternal in man, for Thy kingdom which is in the union of hearts, for the freedom which is of the soul."[2] From this it should not be inferred that Rabindranath has no sympathy with things non-Indian. He is quite sure that the civilisation of the West is as much a creation of the spirit as any other civilisation. Only its soul cannot be grafted on the Indian soul. Radical reformers seem

[1] *Nationalism*, p. 54.

[2] *India's Prayer*.

to think that it is an easy process, as they imagine that India is some recent throw-up from the bottom of the sea, due to a caprice of the earth, with a clean waxen surface ready to receive any impression from the outside. But India is an ancient land with established traditions, honoured throughout recorded history for her spiritual civilisation, for her dignity of soul, for her intense piety, for her valour and chivalry, tolerance and hospitality, and love and peace. All these qualities have become part and parcel of the mentality of the Indian. It is not possible for him to give up what is in his blood and bone. He can only take in the outer and lose the inner. It is easier to acquire the vices of an alien civilisation than to get its virtues. As a matter of fact, contact with the West has disturbed the simple religion and life of the Indian. His intense belief in God, his sense of the strength of holiness and sacrifice, are slowly giving way to materialism and worship of money. The passion for things unseen is being replaced by the fierce eagerness to grow rich. The brows intended to look up to heaven are kissing the dust. The heart to be filled with God is set upon comfort and display. The joy of life and creativeness is yielding to the fever of acquisition and possession. A long purse and a happy home are looked upon as the ultimate destiny of man. People of a country which never spurned poverty are growing afraid to be poor. People who knew how to die for a cause with cheerfulness and calm are growing pale by the fear of death, and loving life even at the sacrifice of their souls. Life is ceasing to be life and is becoming mere existence. It is ceasing to be human and is becoming animal. Men are living for pleasure and not for anything else. Their minds are becoming stunted down, from the shortage of intellectual material. Their souls are shrinking, from the famine of spirit. The materialist influence has been steadily growing, and eating subtly into the very substance of the Indian soul. If Rabindranath is against the political subjection of India, it is not due to any selfish motive. He is afraid of the Western spirit, which is slowly subduing the soul of India and impoverishing her life and spirit. As an instance of how much the present outlook of the Indian is shaped by the West, Rabindranath mentions the fact that the modern

Indian looks to Government for aid in everything. Though hordes of invaders deluged the country, the people of India were little affected by these, as they were administering their own affairs in many spheres. All matters connected with education and sanitation, agriculture and industry were under the control of the people. Government was only a nominal head suspended over the people, and not an organic part of it. So when Government changed hands people did not mind it. But to-day everything is to be granted by Government. Prayers and petitions, memorials and resolutions, pious protests and impotent indignations are the talk of the day. If now Government should change, chaos would prevail. The State which was only a symbol of unity has become the whole body now. This idea that everything should be done by the State is completely materialist, and we have unconsciously adopted it. Judged by the greatest test of the vitality of a nation, namely its capacity for self-sacrifice, it must be said that India is becoming denationalised and devitalised. Those who want us to go the whole length in the imitation of the West are dupes of a delusion.

Rabindranath feels that there is a great difference between the spiritual ideal for which India stands, and the material ideal with which it is in conflict. Through the acceptance of the civilisation of the East, which is religious and not secular, it is easy for us to enter the kingdom of God. Though not exclusively, still mainly, the emphasis in the East is on life and not possession, intuition and not intellect, religion and not science, freedom and not direction. It is because India represents this ideal that Rabindranath is proud to be a son of India. "I shall be born in India again and again; with all her poverty, misery, and wretchedness I love India best."[1]

> Blessed is my birth because I was born in the country, blessed is my life, mother, because I have loved thee.
>
> I do not know if thou hast wealth and riches to be a queen. I know this much that my limbs are cooled as soon as I stand in thy shade.
>
> I know not in what grove blossom flowers that madden the soul with such scents. I know not the sky where the moon rises with such sweet smiles.
>
> My eyes were first opened in thy light, and they will be closed finally upon that very light.

We see that Rabindranath has no sympathy

[1] *Modern Review*, February 1917.

with those who, with a light heart, ridicule everything that is old and established and view the past of India as one unbroken period of inertia and darkness. Nor has he much in common with those who in an easy and careless mood accept with veneration everything old and established, and reject with equal vehemence the new and the untried. But when the educated Indians, carried away by the spirit of innovation, look down upon their more cautious brethren with contempt and ridicule, and view them as the enemies of progress, and when this spirit goes beyond bounds and becomes militant and aggressive, Rabindranath feels it his duty to counsel caution and calm, steadiness and self-examination. He asks them to pause for a moment and reflect on the consequences of what they propose to do. But he is not a conservative who wishes to perpetuate mischievous forms simply because they are picturesque, To him progress and reform consist in conserving the ancient ideals and building upon them. Preserving the soul of the Indian type, we may adopt whatever is good and noble in the West. Rabindranath demands a synthetic integration of the old and the new, the East and the West. "It is idle mendicancy to discard our own and beg for the foreign," while at the same time "it is the abjectness of poverty to dwarf ourselves by rejecting the foreign."[1] Rabindranath remarks that "taking shelter in the dead is death itself, and only taking all the risk of life to the fullest extent is living"[2] India has preserved her vitality because, whenever she came into contact with alien civilisations, she absorbed whatever was great in them without surrendering the fundamentals of her own

[1] *My Interpretation of Indian History.* In his address on the spirit of Japan, Rabindranath says: "I am quite sure that there are men in your country, who are not in sympathy with your inherited ideals; whose object is to gain and not to grow. . . . While I agree with them so far as to say, that the spirit of the race should harmonise with the spirit of the time, I must warn them that modernising is a mere affectation of modernism, just as affectation of poetry is poetising. . . . One must bear in mind that those who have the true modern spirit need not modernise, just as those who are truly brave are not braggarts. Modernism is not in the dress of the European, or in the hideous structures where their children are interned when they take their lessons, or in the square houses with flat, straight wall surfaces pierced with parallel lines of windows where these people are caged in their lifetime; certainly modernism is not in their ladies' bonnets carrying on them loads of incongruities. These are not modern but merely Europe. True modernism is freedom of mind, not slavery of taste. It is independence of thought and action, not tutelage under European schoolmasters. It is science but not its wrong application to life." All this applies *mutatis mutandis* to the modern Indian who wants to transplant European civilisation in Indian soil.

[2] *Nationalism*, p. 53.

type. Whatever we adopt from others we have to adapt ourselves to our needs and to our life. India has her own self-identity, her life and soul. She can grow strong and vigorous not by the mere accumulation of Western forms and modes, but by the assimilation of them all. She should affix the stamp of her genius to whatever she lays her hands upon and accepts, otherwise her work will not be a creation, but a mere repetition. The process of assimilative synthesis has been the characteristic of India from the beginning of her history. When first the original Aryans settled at the foot of the Himalayas, the Dravidian civilisation was indented upon to a large extent. "Let none, however, imagine that non-Aryans have contributed nothing of value to Indian life. The ancient Dravidians were not indeed deficient in civilisation. Contact with them made the Hindu civilisation varied in aspect and deeper in spirit. The Dravidian was no theologian, but an expert in imagination, music, and construction. He excelled in fine art. The pure spiritual knowledge of the Aryans, mingling with the Dravidian's emotional nature and power of æsthetic creation, formed a marvellous compound, which is neither entirely Aryan nor entirely non-Aryan, but Hindu."[1] When later Buddhism became merged in Hinduism, it is the same process. Hinduism has synthesised all the foreign influences which invader after invader has brought to her from outside, and moulded them to its own ideals. India had always welcomed foreign influence. Hinduism has been ever old and ever new. It has been both creative and constructive. The secret of the strength of Hinduism lies in its power of assimilation. "Doubt not the nation's capacity for self-help: know for certain that the time has come. Remember how India has ever kept alive her power of binding together. She has ever established some sort of harmony amidst all kinds of difficulties and conflicts, and hence she has survived till now. I have full faith in that India. Even now that India is slowly building up a marvellous reconciliation of the old order with the new. May each of us consciously join in that work, may we be never misled by dulness or revolt into resisting it."[2] If Indian nationality is to be a live

[1] *Modern Review*, 1913. [2] *Ibid.* June 1913.

spirit and not a dead imitation, then India must build up from within. Her hope lies within herself. The basis and foundation of the great India lies in the recovery of her soul and the regaining of a fresh self-confidence in her own national life. If India recovers her strength of soul and grip of spirituality, which is the secret spring of life, then no power on earth can stand against her newly acquired energy of spirit. If the soul is diseased, then it will inevitably bend in decay and death, however much we might try to prevent it by external means; but if the soul is healthy it will live down disaster, retrieve ruin, and reassert itself in spite of all external opposition. Nothing has power over it. Nothing can stand against the uprush of spirit. The soul of a nation with ideals of spirit cannot be overcome. If this faith possesses the souls of men enduringly, India will "emerge one day."

The Upanishad says: "This self is not to be gained by the weak."[1] This recovery of soul is a hard task. We may have anxious times to go through. For it, it may be, we may have to "give up our father and mother,

[1] *Nāyamātmā balahīnēna labhyah.*

wife and children." To us, with our materialist outlook, the heights to which we may have to mount may seem giddy and dreadful. We may fall—the first climbers are certain to—but such falls are needed for the rise of India. However threatening the idea may appear, it is not impossible. For the spirit of India is not yet dead, though it may have gone to sleep. Her heart has been beating slower and slower, but it has not come to a stop. The flame of spiritual life is kept burning, though dim, all these years of stress and strain. It is this spiritual self-possession, won through ages of mysticism, that has made the Indian civilisation survive the onslaughts of the outside world. Heaven does not send such men as Rabindranath Tagore to undeserving nations. Their presence is a standing proof of the fact that the ideas for which India stands are not eclipsed, and her song not silenced. Great ideas still move her, and are the inspiration of her life and the breath of her poetry. Rabindranath has full faith in the great future of India, and with the burning faith which animates the prophet he speaks out: "Is it impossible to utilise the supreme ideas of the *Panchayagnya* in forming a daily tie between our whole country and every member of our community? Cannot every one of us daily offer one pice or even a handful of rice in the name of our fatherland? Cannot Hinduism bind every one of us, every day of our life, with the direct bond of devotion to India, to *Bharata varsha*, the haunt of our Gods, the hermitage of our ancient Rishis, the nourishing mother of our forefathers? Cannot our relation with our benign fatherland be brought home to every one of us as a particular personal tie?"[1] Rabindranath, with the devouring flame of his patriotism, calls upon his countrymen to strive to create a devotion to the mother country, a sense of pride in its glory, and a passion for its progress.

IV

To offset the invading course of low materialist ideals, the ideals of Indian education

[1] *Modern Review*, June 1913. From this it is obvious that Rabindranath supports the idea of national solidarity. This may seem inconsistent with his criticism of nationalism in the West and his frequent reference to the East as a world of no-nations. What he means is that the East has no nations in the Western sense of the term; it has no organisations of greed and oppression, no machines which suppress all individuality. Eastern peoples are nations as each of them has a soul and a genius. India should develop national unity on the basis of its spiritual vision of freedom and humanity, love and fellowship.

should be changed. The modern educated Indian is a false copy of his Western contemporary. His voice is an echo, his life a quotation, his soul a brain, and his free spirit a slave to things. Rabindranath is so repelled by these modern products that he bursts out: "Ours is truly a God-forsaken country. Difficult indeed is it for us to keep up the strength of our will to do. We get no help in any real sense. We have none within miles of us, in converse with whom we may gain an access of vitality. No one seems to be thinking or feeling or working. Not a soul has any experience of big striving, or of real and true living. They all eat and drink, do their office work, smoke and sleep and chatter nonsensically. When they touch upon emotion they grow sentimental; when they reason they are childish. . . . One yearns for a full-blooded, sturdy, and capable personality; these are all so many shadows, flitting about out of touch with the world."[1] These products of Western education are not persons but shadows. There is neither art in their life nor music in their souls. Modern education has

[1] Letters, *Modern Review*, July 1917.

developed a slave mind. It has succeeded, we may say after Dr. Coomaraswamy, in driving art to museums and picture-galleries, knowledge into libraries and bookstalls, religion to Sundays and scriptures, and music into gramophones and concert halls. The progress of India is not so much in human souls as in bluebooks. The educated Indian is revenging himself on his educator by developing into a cheap and troublesome imitation of himself. He is like a cut flower of humanity without any roots. True education must spring from the deeper side of a man's nature. But now the educated Indian is cut off from his past, and from the immemorial traditions and affections and restraints which bind him to his kin and country. The education which is being given is not that of the whole man. The modern school is a factory "specially designed for grinding out uniform results."[1] Absolutely no account is taken of individual variations. The same method is applied to the mental needs of an infinite variety of minds. There is no freedom for the expansion of soul or the progress of liberal thought. The religious and

[1] *Personality*, p. 114.

the artistic, the moral and the spiritual sides, are drowned in the study of scientific formulas and social laws. The mechanisation of mind and the sterilisation of the intellectual seed-plot are the results of the tyranny of the educational policy. Even from the intellectual point of view the product of this policy does not command respect. We cannot say that he has any enthusiasm for knowledge, or respect for culture, or any motive for independent thought. The scheme of examinations vulgarises his mind. He does not care to know what is true, but what will fetch him marks. Not knowledge for the sake of knowledge, but knowledge for the sake of success at the examinations is the governing principle of his whole study. He has already an eye on his future life, and his ambitions interfere with his studies. He knows that in India there is a career only for mechanics and clerks, and there is not much room for talent to breathe freely. No wonder that he adjusts himself to the conditions. The modern Indian is not taught the profound interpretation of the soul of man enshrined in his great literature. The records of the inner spiritual life of the Indian race are utterly neglected. It is obvious that nothing can so awaken powers, kindle spiritual aspiration, and set souls aquiver as a great literature which describes the highways of the human soul. There cannot be a more potent stimulus or a greater spur to the Indian mind and imagination than her ancient literature, to which the modern educated Indian is a stranger. Indian children are forgetting their past, and they are unable to understand their own nature; and they "stand as barriers choking the stream that flows from the mountain peak of their ancient history," and her future will be deprived of the water of life "that has made her culture so fertile with richness of beauty and strength."[1] The ideal which India possessed in the past should come back in its essence, though not in its entirety. Education should make for the culture of the soul, and not merely for the feeding of intellect or the cramming of memory. "The highest education is that which does not merely give us information but makes our life in harmony with all existence."[2] "The object of education is to give man the unity of truth. Formerly, when life was simple,

[1] *The Spirit of Japan.* [2] *Ibid.* p. 116.

all the different elements of man were in complete harmony. But when there came the separation of the intellect from the spiritual and the physical, the school education put entire emphasis on intellect and the physical side of man. We devote our sole attention to giving children information, not knowing that by this emphasis we are accentuating a break between the intellectual, physical, and the spiritual life."[1] But how is the spiritual life to be cultivated? Not by means of any set lessons about God and His existence, but by allowing the souls to express themselves freely and spontaneously. For no man with a living soul in him will say what the fool saith in his heart, that there is no God. Rabindranath trusts to the instinct of the pupil and the atmosphere of the *Asram* for the kindling of the spiritual aspiration and the development of the spiritual life. "With the breath we draw we must always feel this truth, that we are living in God."[2] In ancient India it was possible, because in the *asram*, which is home, school, temple, and forest rolled into one, the teachers were men who every moment

[1] *The Spirit of Japan*, p. 126. [2] *Ibid.*

felt the presence of God and lived their life in Him. So their pupils felt God as they felt the green of the earth or the blue of the sky. In India the ideal of education has been to instil the vision of the eternal that so the soul might reach its fulness and freedom. Such education, which aims at the emancipation of the soul and the liberation of the human spirit from its trammels, would open the eyes of Indians to the enormous waste of life, health, and spirit, which daily takes place in the country; would reveal to them the complete circumscription of opportunity, and would give them the courage of heart and strength of mind to fight injustice in every form. In his school at Bolpur, which is not only a school of culture but an abode of piety and a school of art, Tagore combines modern methods of education with the ancient Indian ideal of soul-culture. To him the ideal school "must be an *asram* where men have gathered together for the highest end of life, in the peace of nature; where life is not merely meditative but fully awake in its activities, where boys' minds are not perpetually drilled into believing that the ideal of the self-idolatry of the nation is the truest ideal for them to accept; where they are bidden to realise man's world as God's kingdom to whose citizenship they have to aspire; where the sunrise and sunset and the silent glory of the stars are not daily ignored; where nature's festivities of flowers and fruit have their joyous recognition from man; and where the young and the old, the teacher and the student, sit at the same table to partake of their daily food and the food of their eternal life."[1]

Vernaculars should be the medium of education. It cannot be seriously contended that English should become the common language of the whole of India. Even if it is possible, it is doubtful if it is desirable. We cannot hope to develop any great literature in the English tongue. Much of the superficiality of the present-day educated classes, their lack of originality in spite of abundant assimilative genius, are due to the defects of bilingual thinking. "Our foreign learning of to-day remains a thing of the school or college, is kept hung up like a sign-board and does not become a part of our life—or remains in our note-

[1] *The Spirit of Japan*, p. 148.

books and fails to get transcribed into thought and action."[1] Rabindranath thinks that insistence on the learning of English in the early years cuts at the root of all sound educational theory, and introduces a tedium and weariness instead of cheerfulness into the daily routine. He says: "Learning should as far as possible follow the process of eating. When the taste begins from the first bite, the stomach is awakened to its functions before it is loaded, so that its digestive pieces get full play. Nothing like this happens, however, when the Bengali boy is taught in English. The first bite bids fair to wrench loose both rows of teeth like a veritable earthquake in the mouth; and by the time he discovers that the morsel is not of the genus stone but a digestible bonbon, half his allotted span of life is over. While one is choking and spluttering over the spelling and grammar, the inside remains starved, and when at length taste is felt, the appetite has vanished. If the whole mind does not work at the beginning, its full powers remain undeveloped to the end."[2] The poet wrote all his works in Bengalee and later

[1] *Modern Review*, October 1917. [2] *Reminiscences*, p. 59.

translated some of them into English. English with him is only a second language, but in the schools, vernaculars are the second languages. As the vernaculars are not the medium of education, a gulf has opened up between the educated classes and the masses. English education has created an upper class of educated men divorced from the people's outlook. It has given them ideas which they cannot fulfil as they do not know how to fulfil them. The charge often urged that they do not represent the masses is not altogether without foundation. The educated men feel as if they were a class apart. Their traditional ideas are unsettled and their religious beliefs weakened. They have acquired a Eurasian mentality while the large masses are Indian still. In congresses and conferences English is the principal language. Men knowing English are treated with respect and consideration. They are proficient in appealing to Government, while they do not show as much zeal in creating among their countrymen a unity of purpose and will and feeling, which is the more important aim of political endeavour. The true way to touch the heart of the people would be to make vernaculars the means for the spread of knowledge. This is the only way to carry the good tidings to every corner of India. If we do not preserve the sacred Sanskrit and the beautiful vernaculars of India and help them to grow by use and exercise, then the very springs of Indian higher life are destroyed.

The recovery of the religious spirit is necessary for reviving the harmony of art and industry, beauty and use. Machinery is displacing Indian industries; and while Rabindranath is not against the introduction of machinery, still the spirit in which machinery is worked and the results to which it leads call forth his condemnation. In the story of "A Resolve Accomplished," he refers to the displacement of the handloom by the machine in these terms: "A pack of evil spirits, however, advanced from over the sea, and hurled missiles of fire upon the inoffensive loom. They set the demon of hunger in the poor weavers' homes and the whistling of steam sounded like frequent blasts from their horns of victory."[1] While he believes that

[1] *Glimpses of Bengal Life*, by Rajani Ranjan Sen.

industrialism must come to India and should come, he considers that India need not pass through the evils of industrialism. He thinks that Eastern thought can be reconciled with the mechanism of Western civilisation. "In the East we have striven to disregard matter, to ignore hunger and thirst, and so to escape from their tyranny and emancipate ourselves. But that is no longer possible, at least for the whole nation. You in the West have chosen to conquer matter, and the pure task of science is to enable all men to have enough to satisfy their material wants and by subduing matter to achieve freedom for the soul. The East will have to follow the same road and call in science to its aid."[1] It will be weak sentimentalism to recoil with aversion from machinery, which has come to stay in India. What we have to guard ourselves against is the temptation to divorce art from industry. We should see to it that machinery does not make us lose faith in soul and character. If we imitate the West by banishing art from industry, religion from life, then India will have to suffer an age of industrialism, which

[1] *Lectures in America.*

would come with a heavy hand, bringing new fetters and riveting old chains. Hideous slum life, unemployment, long hours of labour, and liquor traffic would all be repeated on the soil of India. But if the Indian view is adopted, that all life, economic, intellectual, and social, should reflect the spirit of religion, then art and industry will go together and India will not suffer from an amoral artless industrialism. The ugliness and dulness, the ignorance and discontent, of the labouring populations are due to the lack of the religious spirit. In ancient India what men made they made well without being conscious of it; for then they had the joy of labour of which art is the expression. Then the creative spirit or the desire for expression was satisfied in all work. Now they have lost the joy in life. The gross vulgarity of manners and bestiality of art are the expression of a wrong state of mind. The god in man is being slowly suppressed by the beast in him. It is because the work that the labourer does is not congenial to him, because it does not exercise his mind and intelligence, that his soul is shrivelled, his life embittered, and his faculty stunted. There is no use in criticising modern Indian art. We should criticise the conditions of life and society that have made it possible. The birds are not to blame if the heat and the dust prevent them from singing their best. No doubt the British Government is doing a great deal in the way of preserving the ancient monuments, etc., but the pity of it is they are trying to preserve the matter while undermining the mind which could create it. The fire is put out while the ashes are collected in the museums. The living faith and the national feeling are steadily losing ground. The creative imagination on which the vitality of art depends is being silenced by the disproportionate cultivation of intellect, which revels in empty formulas and barren concepts. The intellectual stimulus provided by modern education does not give it life. Its result has been to make mind material and the outlook on life grossly commercialistic. Cheapness, utility, and trade-instinct have taken the place of beauty, life, and soul-power. But if the religious Indian remembers that industry must have a soul, that the products of mills and factories should not only be useful but also fine, that they should not only satisfy the material needs of the body but also minister to the spiritual needs of the soul, then art will take its place as a stimulus to national life, and bring beauty into it. "I must ask you to believe," says William Morris, "that every one of the things that go to make up the surroundings among which we live must be either beautiful or ugly, either elevating or degrading to us, either a torment and a burden for the maker of it to make or a pleasure and a solace to him." The simple instinct of man to surround himself with objects from which he could draw delight should be satisfied, but now we are surrounded by useful objects which offend the eyes. The end of industry should be artistic production which will be the expression of the human spirit with its freedom and flow of creativeness. Every worker should realise that he is to contribute to the spiritual welfare of the user and not merely to his bodily needs. Then shall we understand the significance of work for life. Then will labour come to be undertaken with joy, hope, and confidence, and become self-expression. Working his creative impulse, instead of being a task and a drudgery, will become his pleasure and pastime. Organisation, instead of being the killing of the soul, will be the utterance of the inner beauty. "For the rhythm of beauty is the inner spirit whose outer body is organisation."[1]

The modern Indian is forgetting the function of art in life. Art is the great emancipator from the routine of life. It lifts us from the clamorous assaults of sense and frees us from the torrent of external impressions. "A thing of beauty is a joy for ever." It makes us pierce through the veil which hides the eternal within and shows it to us. The present-day art, which has the taint of materialism and which lacks dignity and repose, is a mirror of the present-day soul, which has no centre, no permanent value which it can oppose to the flux of sense. Apart from the satisfaction of animal wants, the modern Indian's life is one continuous hustle and excitement for social success and financial prosperity. He goes about seeing people, and dancing attendance on the powers that be for a title or a ribbon. There are no vacant spaces in his life, but all is one frightful motion due to ambi-

[1] *The Spirit of Japan.*

tion and avarice. Life is stifled and overtasked. Man has time only for animal pleasures and not for divine joy. If he worships anything it is money, which he deifies. He thinks it the only thing that makes life worth living. Valuing money more than art, he lives in the world of actualities and forgets ideals. He feels a stranger in his own home. Can great art be produced in these conditions? Are haste and hustle the atmosphere for the creation of art? The poverty of India is another obstacle. We must cease to work if we would have play; cease to think of life before we can have good life. How can we retain freshness of outlook and perpetual youth when we are so worried with cares and details? Immersed in life, man has no time to think of the unseen, the root and stay of life. Man becomes a piece of clockwork, a machine with some motive-power which is soon exhausted by the work necessary for either keeping the wolf from the door or winning social recognition. A masterpiece of mechanism that man has become, how can he produce any art? It is said that India is progressing. It is admitted that we have much less of chaos and anarchy, much less of thuggism and dacoity, much less of crimes and murders. But we cannot say that the progress has been real or, in the true sense of the word, moral. Seeley quite rightly observes: "A city without picture galleries, theatres, beautiful buildings, a city where no one writes verses or reads them or cares to talk about literary subjects, must, I imagine, be far worse than a dismal place. It need not, perhaps, be an immoral place in the common sense of the word. The average number of thefts and murders committed in it need not be greater than in other places of the same size; but in a high sense of the word I think it must be immoral; the standard will be pitched low; life will be uninteresting and virtue will become languid and, so to speak, unprogressive."[1] Such is life in India, slovenly, disgusting, and joyless. For reviving life and art a religious movement is needed. Religion is the breath of life, and art when it was great blended with religion. India saw beauty as it saw God in every thing, form, expression, and movement. If this spirit is recovered, then all life will become an art,

[1] *Lectures and Essays*, p. 171.

challenging us to develop its artistic possibilities on all sides.

V

Among the national defects which prevent India from rising to her full height are an exaggerated sense of other-worldliness and belief in fatality. We have already noted how the great souls of India, while they develop their spiritual mysticism with concentrated fervour, ignore with equal fulness the practical details of the world. They forget that only human fellowship can make God real to man. "In pleasure and in pain I stand not by the side of man and thus stand by thee."[1] In the art of life Tagore wishes us to practise the synoptic vision of the harmony of the whole and wholeness of personality, not antagonism between parts. Asceticism and mutilation of the body calumniate God, the Author of all being. Insulted nature is taking revenge on us. The retired life of contemplation and devotion should yield to one of sacrifice and devotion. We may say with Emerson that our hands must be in the world of action and our heads

[1] *Gitanjali*, 77.

above the storm. "Give us strength to love, to love fully, our life in its joys and sorrows, in its gains and losses, in its rise and fall. Let us have enough strength to see and hear thy universe and to work with full vigour therein."[1] In mediæval India, religion, to a large extent, was an opiate, a force that made men and women resigned to their sufferings. Rabindranath protests against this world-negating attitude.

> No, my friends, I shall never leave hearth and home, and retire into the forest solitude, if rings no merry laughter in its echoing shade and if the end of no saffron mantle flutters in the wind; if its silence does not deepen my soft whispers.
>
> I shall never be an ascetic.[2]

With Rabindranath, religion becomes the inspiration of everyday life, a force which puts power into the arm of those who fight injustice in the world. His is not the false, abstract, negative asceticism which has had a long vogue in India, but the hard austere asceticism of the saint who, brightened by the beatific vision of a better world to be won here on earth not by renunciation but by pain, struggle, and achievement, works for the welfare of humanity.

[1] *Sādhanā*, p. 133.　　[2] *Gardener*, p. 78.

Belief in karma, interpreted as fatality, has deprived the Indian of spirit and spontaneity, initiative and endeavour. But karma is only a name for man's own past, and man as spirit has control over it.

> Who drives me forward like fate?
> The myself striding on my back.[1]

The drive of doom is only the influence of man's own past. Man is mightier than his karma. While his body and possessions are subject to the law of karma or necessity, the mind of man is free. Man is in bondage so long as he is at the mercy of vain hopes and fears, when he considers himself to have interests and possibilities of his own apart from the whole of which he is a part. He is free when he knows his place in the universe and realises it in his life. His freedom rises or falls according as he is more or less selfless. The spark of divinity in man is the sign of his freedom, and fatality, in the words of Romain Rolland, is the "excuse of souls without a will." Rabindranath writes: "Asks the Possible to the Impossible, 'Where is your dwelling-place?' 'In the dreams of the impotent,'

[1] *Stray Birds.*

comes the answer."[1] Man is the captain of his soul, and it is foolish to give up attempts in the belief that all is due to karma.

The song of Rabindranath is a call to national consciousness and an inspiration to national devotion. He asks us to employ to greater purpose the most precious energies of the Indian soul. Of all the energies of the world, the greatest are those which reside within a people's heart and character. He calls upon Indians to pour out their energies into the country's cause without surrendering themselves to the temptations of false asceticism and fatality.

VI

This sketch would be incomplete without an account of Rabindranath's views about the political condition of India. With all the advantages of good government India cannot be said to be free. For freedom means not estrangement from life or killing of faculty, but the enlargement of self, the expansion of personality, and the utmost possible extension of faculty and desire. This we can have only

[1] *Stray Birds*, 129.

if we have the right of self-government, for "the right of being one's own master is the greatest of man's rights."[1] But India which is deprived "of the discipline of self-government and means of self-defence" is not free.[2] For the present condition of India, she is as much responsible as Britain. There is such a thing as the logic of history. The world is not in the hands of blind inconsequence. If nations suffer, it is not without reason. The fall of India is due to the narrow outlook of the average Indian. The clash of castes and creeds, the atmosphere of hate and prejudice, the indifference to the disinherited of the earth, the waste of the spiritual wealth of the country, the waging of war on the ancient dead of India, have all contributed to the fall of India. The people gave up their rich and spiritual heritage and became intensely selfish, and the present distress is the outcome. India shall not win freedom unless and until she casts off her materialism and selfishness. "So long as we, out of personal and collective ignorance, cannot treat our countrymen properly like men,

[1] "Thou shalt obey," *Modern Review*, September 1917.

[2] *Sādhanā*, p. 109.

so long as our landlords regard their tenants as a mere part of their property, so long as the strong in our country will consider it the eternal law to trample on the weak, the higher castes despise the lower as worse than beasts, even so long we cannot claim gentlemanly treatment from the English as a matter of right, even so long we shall fail to truly waken the English character, even so long will India continue to be defrauded of her due and humiliated."[1] The greatest enemies of nations are not their foreign foes, but the forces that dwell within their borders. From these nations have to be saved. The real obstacles to Indian progress lie in regions where the British Government has no sway. The blind superstitions, the deification of customs, the ancient institutions which make for discord, are responsible for the present degenerate condition of India. To the question, Why is India only a dependency and not a partner? why is she merely in the group without being of it? why is she a veritable pariah among the nations of the British Empire? Tagore's answer would be, Why are

[1] *The Future of India.*

the forty million untouchables kept down by the people of India? why are they in Hinduism but still not of it? why are they considered pariahs among the peoples of India? India is only reaping the fruits of her past karma. As India treats her lower classes, so will conquering nations treat India. Till caste prejudice and religious pride disappear from India, she will have no right to complain of the race-hatred and race-prejudice of the outside world. We cannot ask for absolute political freedom so long as we welcome cruel tyranny in social life. We cannot break life into fractions. We cannot say we shall be free in religion, fight for freedom in politics, but be enslaved in social life. Ages of suffering are the means by which God helps nations to recover their souls. Though the stars are always in the heavens, yet man sees them only at night. The misfortune that has overtaken India will help her to look up to the stars of eternity, which shine as brightly in the heaven above as in the heart below. The hard school of misfortune is needed to tear India from the false idols of commerce, luxury, and pleasure, and bring her back to God. Suffering is the penalty which

India has to pay for the corruption of centuries. Through it the soul of India is being glorified and her spirit regenerated. Under the spur of sorrow, suffering, and subjection nations like individuals rise to their spiritual heights. God is chastising the people of India and calling them to repentance. Contact with the West has made India become conscious of her weakness and unworthiness. Like St. Peter of old, India now hears the cock crow and weeps saying, "Lord, I have denied thee!" She is reawakening, is learning the causes of her decadence and coming to believe in the truth of her ancient ideals and inspiration.

"To-day India is on every side defrauding and humiliating herself in scripture, religion, and society; she is not awakening her own soul by means of truth and sacrifice, therefore she is not getting from others what she otherwise might have had. Therefore the union with the West is not becoming complete in India; that union is not bearing full fruit, but only giving us shame and pain."[1] Rabindranath is not a cynic to laugh at the condition of India. He is dreadfully earnest, and has

[1] *The Future of India.*

neither the time nor the mood for cynicism. The undertone of sorrow in his writings is due to the consciousness that India is not doing her share. The present condition of India makes his heart sick. "Our endeavours after political agitation seemed to me unreal to the core and pitifully feeble in their utter helplessness. I felt that it is a blessing of Providence that begging should be an unprofitable profession, and that only to him who hath shall be given. I said to myself that we must seek for our own inheritance and with it buy our true place in the world." What is that inheritance? "The ideals of simplicity of life, clarity of spiritual vision, purity of heart, harmony with the universe, and consciousness of the infinite personality in all creation."[1] He knows what conditions are to be reckoned with, what factors are operating to thwart the bright burning of the flame of spirit. India with the colossal poverty, illiteracy, and ignorance of the masses, the rising materialism and the waning idealism of the classes, the gradual impoverishment of spirit, the petty dissensions and quarrels, the low level of

[1] *Shantiniketan*, Introduction, pp. 2, 3.

sanitation and education, which make themselves felt when a famine or an epidemic visits the country, is a sight which will make the most cheerful temper surrender itself to gloom. The seeming pessimism of Rabindranath's writings is due to his realisation of the forces working against the spiritual revival. He has no doubt about the great future of India when she realises the promise of her past, but he is sorry that it has not come yet. The vein of sadness is due to this disappointment. Rabindranath has visions of the future inspired by the story of the past, but the present does not seem to contain the promise of the coming era. There is the indifference to the things of spirit; the silence in the temple of God. There is the altar yet standing but broken and profaned. India once the home of spirit is now flooded with materialism, once glorious and brilliant in power and life is now lost in inertia and egotism. We may go round and round, but we shall not catch any generous sympathy or pure enthusiasm or earnest spiritual aspiration. Prosaic calculation and selfishness have invaded all things and made mankind isolated, degraded and deformed. Looking at the desert of the world around with its spiritual solitude, his heart sinks with the burning weight on it. Rabindranath, who is of imagination all compact, feels that a religious revival will lift India from her present decadence. It alone can bring new life where life is becoming extinct, and new hope where hope is being abandoned. As he brings us the glad tidings of deliverance, his message is one of joy and hope, courage and optimism.

VII

Rabindranath is glad that India has come temporarily under the sway of Britain, for the impulse to national life and regeneration first came through this contact. A general questioning in all matters, social, moral, and religious, has arisen. People are asking what it is that is wrong with the Indian civilisation which it has been obtaining that has made it a failure in certain respects. What is it that has betrayed India into its present condition of economic poverty and political subjection? Contact with the West has resulted in unrest in all matters, and has afforded an opportunity for the recasting of some of the old formulas of the Indian civilisation. Rabindranath recognises the good work done by Britain in India. He is sure that if India should be subject to any foreign domination, it were better British than any other. Britain has created an efficient though costly administration, an effective reign of law which has given security to life and property, and thus laid the foundations of national progress and unity. To Britain, India owes her political ideal of freedom. When Britain stepped into India, she consciously or unconsciously set in motion forces which will not cease to operate until freedom becomes an accomplished fact. "Recently the British have come from the West and occupied a chief place in Indian history. This event is not uncalled for or accidental. India would have been shorn of its fulness if it had missed contact with the West. The lamp of Europe is still burning; we must kindle our old extinguished lamp at that flame and start again on the road of time. We must fulfil the purpose of our connection with the English. This is our task to-day in the building up of great India." The contact with Britain has led to the liberation of spirit and emancipation of man. This great task is to be carried out to its logical conclusion. There is no use in liberating spirit only to kill it. Spiritual liberation is the basic principle of political freedom, and one means the other. England has to an extent contributed to the first, but has yet to grant the second. She has created ideals of citizenship, patriotism, and political freedom which she is bound to fulfil. There is no use in complaining, in the opinion of Rabindranath, that responsible government by the Indians cannot replace good government by the British, as the peoples are politically backward and would make mistakes. The spirit of European civilisation has taught us to reply to this charge thus: "The making of mistakes is not such a great disaster as the deprivation of the right of being one's own master. We can only arrive at truth if we are left free to err. We have yet more to say; we can remind our rulers that though they may now be proudly driving the automobile of democracy, the creaking of the old parliamentary cart, when it first started on its journey in the night, as it jerked its way from the rut of one precedent to another, did not sound exactly like the music of a triumphal progress. It had not always the benefit of a steam-roller-smoothed road. How it used to sway from this interest to that, now of the king, now of the church, now of the landlord, now of the brewer, through faction, corruption, brawling and ineptitude! Was there not even the time when the attendance of its members had to be secured under threat of penalty? And talking of mistakes, what a dismal tale could be unfolded of the mistakes the mother of parliaments has made, beginning from the time of its old relations with Ireland and America down to its recent action in the Dardanelles and Mesopotamia—to say nothing of the not inconsiderable list which might be compiled for India alone. . . . Self-government not only leads to efficiency and a sense of responsibility, but it makes for an uplift of the human spirit. It is only when those who are confined within the parochial limits of village or community—are given the opportunity of thinking and acting imperially that they will be able to realise humanity in its larger sense. For want of this opportunity every person in this country remains a lesser man; . . . so in spite of all the risk of error or mischance we must have self-government." This and this alone is the sovereign cure of all the national distempers of India. "The Englishman may point to his history and tell us: 'This great price of self-government have I earned only after many a struggle and with infinite toil and trouble.' I admit it. Each pioneer race has arrived at some particular truth through much sorrow, error, and sacrifice. But those who follow after have not to tread the same long path of tribulation. What it took ages of shower and sunshine for Europe to mature, Japan was able to transplant in no time, roots and all, to her own soil. . . . So if in our character the qualities necessary for successful self-government appear to be in defect, it is all the more reason that practice in that art should be the sooner commenced. . . . Had it been true that men must first deserve and then desire, then no people in the world would ever have attained freedom. The West boasts of democracy to-day. I have no wish to stir up the repulsive mire which is still so plentiful beneath the surface glamour of the Western peoples. Had there been some paramount power to rule, that, while such a state of things prevail, no democracy is to step into its rights, then not only would all the foulness have remained where it is, but all hope of its ever being cleansed away would vanish. So in our social life and our individual outlook there are no doubt blemishes. But still we must be our own masters. The great festival of man is in progress, but in no country are all its lamps ablaze—nevertheless the festivity proceeds apace. If our lamp has gone out for some little while, what harm if we light its wick at Britain's flame? While it would not diminish Britain's lustre, it would add to the world's illumination."[1] It is Rabindranath's feeling that India would progress far faster if the people were granted self-government. There is the example of Japan, and there is nothing to prevent India from progressing in the same way. If the representatives of Britain in India do not welcome the signs of growth and change in men's ideas but rather try to suppress them with a high hand, even that is necessary, Rabindranath thinks, for the advancement of India, for he says:

---

[1] "Thou shalt obey," *Modern Review*, September 1917.

The more they tighten their bands, the more will our bands snap; the more their eyes redden, the more will our eyes open.

Now it is time for you to work and not to dream sweet dreams, and the more they roar, the quicker and better will our sleepiness be cured.

Persecutions do not crush convictions and faith but help to foster them. The repressive measures create a feeling of suspicion and distrust in the rulers. The feeling of concord between the two peoples is broken down instead of being allowed to grow into a reasonable harmony. The result is a growing bitterness and a sense of injustice. Rabindranath says: "Extremism is wofully wrong as a policy of Government. The high road of law may sometimes prove a roundabout way of reaching the goal, but, like riding rough-shod over Belgium's rights, the extremism of shortening the legitimate road is never seemly."[1]

Rabindranath firmly believes that Britain will grant to India self-government. She knows, and the European War is reminding her of it, that if empire becomes the dominion of the subject races it cannot last long; if it means the commonwealth of the free then

[1] *Modern Review*, December 1917.

it has a chance. Britain is fighting for this latter conception against the Central Powers which stand for world dominion or downfall. Universal dominion is an idle dream. Empire must have a moral basis. It is a spiritual entity. The mission of Britain is to work the greatest experiment of the world, namely, establish a commonwealth of free nations, belonging to different races, creeds, and religions. It is this spiritual purpose that binds the different peoples of the Empire to-day in fighting the opposite principle. Power is not the one thing great about the British regime. There are historic ideals for which Britain stands, and the British rule in India should not give the lie to those ideals. It will be an insult to the free peoples of the British commonwealth to tell them that they are in India to hold Indian peoples subject. The revolution in Russia has proved that a Government, however strong and powerful it may be, cannot defy and ignore the general will of the nation. What has been proved to be a dead superstition in Europe cannot be a live reality in Asia, though ideas take a long time to travel from Europe to Asia. The inevitable will come, and it shall be the proud privilege of Britain to guide India to her destiny. What India wants at the present moment is not carping criticism or commercial exploitation, but intelligent sympathy and practical guidance. If Britain gives this, she will be repaid a thousandfold materially and spiritually; if she does not, it will be a betrayal of her trust, a crime against civilisation and a sin against humanity. It will be a disaster if the British connection with India breaks up, for that would be the admission of defeat of reason on both sides. Such a catastrophe only means the failure of reason and the collapse of understanding between the two nations. But so long as there is statesmanship on either side, it will be averted. Rabindranath hopes that the union between England and India will be a permanent one. In connection with nationalism in the West, he observes: "Our only intimate experience of the nation is the British nation, and so far as government by the Nation goes, there are reasons to believe that it is one of the best. Then, again, we have to consider that the West is necessary to the East. We are complementary to each other, because of our different outlooks upon life, which have given us different aspects of truth. Therefore if it be true that the spirit of the West has come upon our field in the guise of a storm, it is, all the same, scattering living seeds that are immortal. And when in India we shall be able to assimilate in our life what is permanent in the Western civilisation, we shall be in the position to bring about a reconciliation of those two great worlds. Then will come to an end the one-sided dominance which is galling. What is more, we have to recognise that the history of India does not belong to one particular race, but it is the history of a process of creation to which various races of the world contributed—the Dravidians and the Aryans, the ancient Greeks and the Persians, the Muhammadans of the West and those of Central Asia. Now that at last has come the turn of the English to bring to it the tribute of their life, we neither have the right nor the power to exclude them from their work of building the destiny of India."[1] Rabindranath feels it his duty to promote this union in every way, and he is up against either

[1] *Modern Review*, June 1917.

party, Britain or India, who behaves in a manner unworthy of the great purpose for fulfilling which they are brought together. Loyalty to the ideals of the British Empire requires that we should remind our rulers of their duty when they fail to see it. His silent and emphatic though dignified protest against the ill-treatment accorded to Indians in Canada, by refusing to set foot on Canadian soil, shows how deep his convictions about the self-respect of Indians are. He does not want them to eat dirt, or pocket insults lying down, or lick the hand that strikes.

Let us know that Thy light grows dim in the heart that bears
its insult of bondage,
That the life, when it becomes feeble, timidly yields Thy
throne to untruth;
For weakness is the traitor who betrays our soul.[1]

VIII

Before we conclude the chapter, we shall consider Rabindranath's views about the ways and means to be adopted for the regeneration of the country. This question is important, as gross misconceptions prevail on the point. It

[1] *India's Prayer.*

is said that Rabindranath's song has been the inspiration to anarchist activities, and is not altogether out of sympathy with the "flirtations with China, Japan and America" of which we sometimes hear from the foreign papers. Strange to say, the opposite view prevails in some quarters in India, where it is urged that Rabindranath has given up his old nationalist attitude. Let us make his position clear.

Rabindranath has no sympathy with the moderates of the Congress party whose political faith is symbolised by the mid-Victorian catchwords of Rationalism and Enlightenment, Progress and Liberty, and whose method is that of peaceful constitutional agitation through the press and the platform. Their attitude to the ancient spirit of India is one of indifference, if not contempt. They talk glibly of Mill and Morley, Burke and Bright, and would be pleased if the rest of India followed them in imitating the Western forms without taste or talent. As their programme is without any spiritual foundation, it does not catch. Rabindranath thinks that the moderates have developed mendicancy in politics into a fine art. The followers of this "begging method" do not have any clear ideas about the future of the country, do not know what paths lead to success, and even if they know, have not the courage to pursue them. The extremists are not the bomb-throwers and the train-wreckers but the advocates of independence of action. While the moderates feel that by talk, persuasion, and such other cheap and easy methods, the political aim can be attained, the extremists are of opinion that without risk and suffering nothing great can be realised. These have a sincere desire to face the issues and think out the problems, and shrink from consoling themselves with comfortable illusions. It is their contention that political problems cannot be solved by a philosophy of phrases. While the moderates try to persuade the rulers by argument, the extremists feel that earnest spiritual work would convince the rulers of the justice of their cause. These turn from shams to realities, and appeal to men of fire and character and demand from them sacrifice of life and home, property and possession for the sake of the country. They also adopt constitutional agitation, but in a bold and strong-nerved manner. But even this school errs, as it forgets that the problem of India is not merely a political one but a problem of life on all its sides. "They did not recognise the patent fact that there were causes in our social organisation which made the Indian incapable of coping with the alien."[1] He asks: "What should we do if, for any reason, England was driven away? We should simply be victims for other nations. The thing we in India have to think of is this—to remove those social customs and ideals which have generated a want of self-respect and a complete dependence on those above us—a state of affairs which has been brought about entirely by the domination in India of the caste system and the blind and lazy habit of relying upon the authority of traditions that are incongruous anachronisms in the present age."[2] To Rabindranath the caste system of India is as mischievous in its effects as the nation of the West. Both are mechanical organisations dead and wooden, inelastic and soulless. His desire is that all servants of India should be dominated by the

[1] *Nationalism*, p. 113.

[2] *Ibid.*

constructive ideal of spiritual freedom, and with this in view should try to rescue the people from despotism, civic, social, and political.

In a country aspiring for a new life, where there is a general yearning for a brighter world and a purer sky, the passions of men assume different forms. While there are people fearful of violent conduct, there are others who gladly court it. Some of those who belong to the latter category are the unfortunate and misguided youths who resort to political crime, in their blind passion to burst asunder the chains that bind the nation. A pessimistic view of the situation breeds in them distrust in right and justice; and cheap compromises of adventure and mistaken notions of cross roads to success commend themselves. Lover of straight conduct that Rabindranath is, he passionately pleads against this school of thought. "I have consistently urged this one thing, that the wages of wrongdoing are never found to be worth while in the long run, for the debt of sin always ends by becoming the heavier. I emphatically assert that the extremism which is neither decent, nor legal, nor open, which means forsaking the straight road and taking to tortuous paths in the hope of sooner gaining a particular end, is always utterly reprehensible." He impresses on the people of India with all the force at his command that there is no short cut to political freedom through sin and crime, but only a royal road through strength and suffering. A straight line is the shortest which can be drawn between two given points not only in space and geometry but also in spirit and life. Curved lines may for a time seem to be shorter, but ultimately they would reveal their own inordinate length. For a time we may think ourselves victorious in creating victims, but victories and victims do not lead to triumph. We may achieve our aim, but it will not last long. Virtue which means sacrifice is the only path to salvation. Stern worship of morality in scorn of all expedients is the only way to life. In the nature of things there is no compromise between good and evil, right and wrong, truth and falsehood. We cannot temper the one with the other. All our actions are under the inexorable dominion of logic. There is such a thing as karma, which we cannot violate with impunity. Every crime will be followed by its expiation. Every violation of rights carries along with it inevitable consequences of strife and suffering which none may prevent; every offence committed generates an amount of immorality which undermines the energy and virtue of the national heart. The moral law holds that when we strike others, that blow comes back to ourselves. Corruption leads to death and not to a new life. Many a resplendent youth, good and devoted to the cause of truth, will by the adoption of violent anarchism grow weak and brutal, for sooner or later the moral crisis comes, when the light that inspires courage and confidence, that strengthens the soul to service and sacrifice, is put out for ever. The vision is darkened by doubt and distrust, the soul poisoned and therefore deadened, and the sacred cause weakened, if not shattered. The high mission confided by God to the care of India cannot be accomplished through walking in crooked ways and adopting false doctrines of expediency, but can be fulfilled only through the worship of eternal truth and the practice of austere virtue, by the sweat of the soul and the sacrifice of the body. Let us not desire to worship falsehood. Let us not seek to sully the whiteness of our souls by acquiring faith in political machiavellism or Jesuitical opportunism. Let us not introduce the gnawing worm of immorality into the soul of our sacred cause. Let us believe that defeat is nobler than dishonour, suffering than infliction of suffering, sorrow than hatred. Let us learn to suffer without hate and sacrifice without despair. Let not the soul be bent to any other authority than that of righteousness which is everlasting, like the mountains. Rabindranath abhors all forms of terrorism and summons his countrymen to work for the regeneration of India, strong in the possession of a pure and stainless conscience. It is his earnest wish that the new patriotic impulse which is a powerful element in the life of young India should be kept pure and clean from being mixed up with any taint of crime or unworthy affection.

While Rabindranath protests against the rage for destruction which has captured a few stray youths in the country, he points out that the tendency is due to the influence of the West. India's religion has always stood for the right. Unrighteous methods may yield us temporary success, but ultimate ruin is inevitable. The Indian Scriptures declare "Men flourish by unrighteousness. In unrighteousness appears their welfare, by unrighteousness they overthrow their enemies, but they are destroyed at the root." The history of the "progressive" nations of the world teaches the Indian youth that all is fair in love and war and diplomacy. He learns that the honour of nations stands rooted in dishonour. He finds that the stern facts of history are contempt for moral law, disregard of human life and indifference to the rights of weak nations. Calculations of diplomacy seem to inspire the practical morality of rising nations which, time and again, have bought and sold, neglected and despised, betrayed and subjugated the weak peoples of the earth. He sees that even in free countries there are miserable squabbles of parties and factions, struggles of states and individuals desirous of power. If with all these they are successful, he infers that success is the result of unscrupulousness. History seems to him to be a register of crimes and misdeeds, and he asks, Why should we not make history in the way it is made? If politically free countries open men's letters,—"a practice near of kin to picking men's pockets" (Carlyle),—break seals, violate secrets and trample on the holy privacy of personality, and if no just retribution has overtaken them, he is inclined to throw overboard the teachings of his scriptures and doubt the very existence of the moral law. Rabindranath says: "We are ashamed of the methods by which some of our youths have attempted to get rid of the obstacles to their country's progress. We are all the more ashamed of it because the idea of the divorce of expediency from Right was taught us by the West. The open and secret lies of diplomacy, the open and secret robberies sanctioned by State craft, are looked upon in the West as the inevitable alloy in the gold which serves to strengthen the metal. Thus have we come to learn that it is foolish and feeble—mere silly sentimentalism—to allow Righteousness to bother and worry where patriotic self-interest shows the way."[1] In this way, the Indian ideals of the inviolability of right, the sanctity of soul and respect for property, have met with defeat, in the struggle with the Western, in the minds of our young. It is high time for nations to repudiate the immoral distinction between private and public morality, and declare with Burke that the principles of true politics are those of morality enlarged. Rabindranath protests against the breaking of life into distinct compartments with separate ideals. We cannot say that family life is one thing, commercial business another, and international politics a third. It may be that the civilisation of Europe practises this compartmental division, but India should withstand the temptation to pay Europe back in her own coin. We should not "imitate Europe in one of her worst features which comes out in her behaviour to people whom she describes as yellow or red, brown or black,"[2] and thus lose faith in God and man, truth and moral law. It is incorrect to think that the West has gained her present eminence by

[1] *Nationalism*, p. 87.

[2] *Ibid.*

the adoption of unscrupulousness. There is a living soul in the Western civilisation which rebels against that deep distrust in man, that cynical contempt for his sacred rights which find expression in the policies of Governments which do not hesitate to break faith and violate rights to gain their selfish ends. The greatness of Europe is due not so much to her perfection of power as to her reverence for unselfish ideals.[1]

It is necessary for a good Government to devise ways and means by which the enthusiasm, energy and power of sacrifice of the nation can be wisely directed. For enthusiasm unregulated by reason, and rooted in despair touches the confines of madness, a result undesirable in the interests of the rulers as well as of the ruled. The devotion to what they consider the right, the power of complete self-surrender and fearless acceptance of death and danger of these extremists can be turned into valuable assets of the country. And it is the duty of a Government interested in putting down political crime to open out paths by which whatever is noble

[1] See *Nationalism*, p. 89.

can be turned to good account. For it is when there are no open avenues to the service of the country that secret and tortuous paths are pursued and hidden and unknown Gods worshipped. Life is movement, and we cannot deny movement. If we stop it in its usual course it seeks other outlets, and in so doing bursts and explodes. The soul is meant for freedom and joy of creation. All the powers in the world cannot arrest the restless search for freedom, the cry of life or the hurrah for existence. "It is not enough to keep open only the avenues to clerical employment in any comprehensive scheme of Imperial Government,—if no road be left for adventurous daring the soul of man will pine for deliverance, and secret passages still be sought, of which the pathways are tortuous and the end unthinkable."[1]

[1] *Reminiscences*, p. 143.

CHAPTER V

THE MESSAGE OF RABINDRANATH TAGORE TO THE WORLD

I

I dreamed in a dream I saw a city invincible to the attacks
of the whole of the rest of the earth ;
I dreamed that was the new city of friends.
Nothing was greater there than the quality of robust love, it
led the rest.
It was seen every hour in the actions of the men of that city,
And in all their looks and words.

WHITMAN.

But what wealth then shall be left us
When none shall gather gold
To buy his friend in the market,
And pinch and pine the sold?

Nay what save the lovely city,
And the little house on the hill,
And the wastes and the woodland beauty,
And the happy fields we till;

And the homes of ancient stories,
The tombs of the mighty dead;
And the wise men seeking out marvels,
And the poet's teeming head;

And the painter's hand of wonder;
And the marvellous fiddle-bow,
And the banded choirs of music:
All those that do and know.

WILLIAM MORRIS.

WE have incidentally referred to Rabindranath's views about the spirit and the ideal which animate the West. It is not true to say that Rabindranath is blind to the virtues of the West or the faults of the East. As an ideal servant of truth and freedom he takes up arms against all shams, Eastern or Western. Rabindranath admits that he was struck by the spirit of social service prevailing in the West. He says: "It was an inspiration to me."[1] He has only praise for the Western ideals of law, order, and freedom. "Through the smoke of cannons and dust of markets, the light of her moral nature has shone bright, whose foundation lies deeper than social conventions and whose province of activity is world-wide. . . . Europe has been teaching us the higher obligations of public good above those of the family and the clan, and the sacredness of law, which makes society independent of caprice, securing for it continuity of

[1] *Modern Review*, 1913, p. 438. See *Nationalism*, p. 68.

progress, and guarantees justice to all men in all positions in life. Above all things Europe has held high before our minds the banner of liberty through centuries of martyrdom and achievement—liberty of conscience, liberty of thought and action, liberty in the ideas of art and literature."[1] In another connection we have noticed how Rabindranath is thankful to the West for the spread of these ideals in the East.

II

The Western civilisation is more mechanical than spiritual, more political than religious, more mindful of power than of peace. This political tendency is expressing itself in many ways. The woman problem is one symptom of it as the European War is another. Rabindranath devotes a chapter in his *Personality* to the problem of the woman. Of the two aspects of life, rest and movement, or being and becoming, the woman has the being aspect predominating in her nature. To the woman belongs domestic life and everything which is personal and human. She takes no real

[1] *The Spirit of Japan.*

interest in the things themselves; her interest is for the sake of the son or the father or the husband. "Wherever there is something which is concretely personal and human, there is woman's world. The domestic world is the world where every individual finds his worth as an individual, therefore his value is not the market value, but the value of love; that is to say, the value that God in his infinite mercy has set upon all his creatures. This domestic world has been the gift of God to woman."[1] Indian thought compares the relationship of man and woman to that of subject and object, form and matter, Purusha and Prakriti. They are organically related as the complementary functions of one whole. Most of the present-day discussions assume that man and woman are alike in everything but sex, like white and black balls which differ only in colour. But there are basic differences which make the analogy unsound. Man and woman are not copies of each other but mutual supplements. Sentiment, feeling, and emotion predominate in woman, while thought, reflection, and composure characterise man. The joys of passivity

[1] *Personality*, p. 177.

and surrender are the woman's, while those of activity and energising are the man's. The woman is made for marriage, while man is made for business. If the man idles away at home, he is said to be unemployed; if the woman does not marry, she is unemployed.

At the present day, woman is being carried away by the intoxication of power. She does not feel that her vocation lies at home. She is restless. She fears marriage and maternity. She is struggling against man's monopoly of business. She is unsexing herself by seeking situations in shops and stations, factories and offices. She is trying to imitate man, and make her life artificial and unnatural. She is craving to acquire man's character and position in public life. The true woman will have neither the desire nor the capacity for it. The yearning for marriage is rooted in the woman's heart. Let us hear what a woman says: "There is not one woman in a million who would not be married if . . . she could have a chance. How do I know? Just as I know that the stars are now shining in the sky, though it is high noon. I never saw a star at noonday, but it is the nature of the stars to shine in the sky and of the sky to hold its stars."[1]

The rebellion of the woman is to be ultimately traced to the masculine character of the present civilisation. It is one of power and movement. "It is a civilisation of power, in which woman has been thrust aside."[2] Man is responsible for the unrest of woman. "But because men in their pride of power have taken to deriding things that are living, and relationships that are human, a large number of women are screaming themselves hoarse to prove that they are not women, that they are true where they represent power and organisation. In the present age they feel that their pride is hurt when they are taken as mere mothers of the race, as the ministers to the vital needs of its existence, and to its deeper spiritual necessity of sympathy and love."[3] Due to the over-busy-ness of man, the woman's world has been getting thinner and thinner. "In its inordinate lust for power and wealth it has robbed woman of the most part of her world, and the home is every day being crowded out by the office." There is hardly any room

[1] Gail Hamilton. [2] *Personality*, p. 172. [3] *Ibid.* p. 129.

for woman in life now. As man puts obstacles and hindrances in the way of woman's free development, she calls for emancipation. As man insults woman, woman is taking vengeance on man. In the modern civilisation the being or the foundational aspects of life are lost sight of, and so "it has lost its balance and it is moving by hopping from war to war." To bring it back to its balance, "woman must step in and impart its life-rhythm to this reckless movement of power." To the true woman the individual is sacred, more sacred than armies and navies, shops and factories. When woman exercises her function in life then will man learn that love is of more value than power. For the woman to acquire her true place the economic civilisation based on competition should give place to a spiritual one based on co-operation. Then shall the meek inherit the earth.

III

The European War—which is another name for hell raging on earth—has pained the poet to the quick and confirmed his view of the spiritual destitution of Europe. His heart is filled with anguish at the colossal waste of life, and a cry of compassion bursts from his lips. "When, mad in their mirth, they raised dust to soil thy robe, O Beautiful, it made my heart sick."[1] The bleeding of the body of God pierced him to the quick. Unrighteous dealing and an aggressive spirit of nationalism are the causes of the European cataclysm. It is Rabindranath's opinion that Europe is now reaping reward for that organised greed called nationalism. "In this War the death-throes of the nation have commenced. It is the fifth act of the tragedy of the unreal. . . . There is a moral law in this world which has its application both to individuals and organised bodies of men. You cannot go on violating these laws in the name of your nation, yet enjoy their advantage as individuals. We may forget truth for our convenience, but truth does not forget us. Prosperity cannot save itself without moral foundation. Until man can see the gaping chasm between his full storehouse and his humanity, until he can feel the unity of mankind, the kind of barbarism which you call

[1] *Fruit-Gathering*, XXXVI.

civilisation will exist." Europe has sown the wind and must reap the whirlwind. Matter is enthroned; science has become the ally of destruction, and in fury of greed one nation is pitilessly destroying another.

All the black evils in the world have overflowed their
banks,

. . . . .

The heat growing in the heart of God for ages—
The cowardice of the weak, the arrogance of the strong,
the greed of fat prosperity, the rancour of the wronged,
pride of race, and insult to man—
Has burst God's peace, raging in storm.[1]

The War is a sign that the Western civilisation is dead and not alive, inert and not alert, mechanical and not spiritual. It looks upon man as a machine and not a soul. It stands for matter with its automatism and not life with its joy. It exalts intellect at the expense of intuition and soul. "Thus man with his mental and material power far outgrowing his moral strength is like an exaggerated giraffe whose head has suddenly shot up miles away from the rest of him, making normal communication difficult to establish. Its greedy head, with its huge dental organisation, has been munching

[1] *Fruit-Gathering*, LXXXIV.

all the topmost foliage of the world, but the nourishment is too late in reaching his digestive organs, and his heart is suffering from want of blood."[1] Rabindranath burns with indignation when he reflects on the spirit of the present European civilisation. "The vital ambition of the present civilisation of Europe is to have the exclusive possession of the devil. All her armaments and diplomacy are directed upon this one object. But these costly rituals for the invocation of the evil spirit lead through a path of prosperity to the brink of cataclysm. The furies of terror which the West has let loose upon God's world come back to threaten herself and goad her into preparations of more and more frightfulness. This gives her no rest, and makes her forget all else but the perils that she causes to others and incurs herself. To the worship of this devil of politics she sacrifices other countries as victims. . . . After centuries of civilisation, nations fearing each other like the prowling wild beasts of the night-time; shutting their doors of hospitality; combining only for purpose of aggression or defence; hiding in

[1] *Nationalism*, pp. 35-36.

the holes their trade secrets, State secrets, secrets of their armaments, making peace-offerings to each other's barking dogs with the meat which does not belong to them; holding down fallen races which struggle to stand upon their feet; with their right hand dispensing religion to weaker peoples while robbing them with their left—is there anything in this to make us envious?"[1] All the evils of the Western civilisation can be ultimately traced to the false spirit of nationalism. The Westerns bow down before the false God, "that dominant intellectual abstraction which you call a nation." Nationality is not in itself bad, but when it is interpreted in a false, selfish, and aggressive sense, then it becomes an evil principle. As Mr. G. Lowes Dickinson observes: "Nationality is a Janus, facing both ways. So far as it stands for the right of a people to govern itself, it stands for freedom. So far as it stands for the ambition to govern other people, or to destroy them or to shape them into an alien mould, it stands for domination. Nationality is respectable only when it is on the defence, when it is waging

[1] *Nationalism*, pp. 83-84.

wars of liberation it is sacred; when those of domination it is accursed."[1] In the West Nationalism is interpreted in a small and selfish sense. It develops a narrow devotion to one's own country and encourages an exclusive patriotism. "Every nation overestimates itself; without this feeling of itself it would also lack the consciousness of being a community; as Fichte truly said, a nation cannot dispense with arrogance."[2] Religion and morality do not make such a strong appeal as the feeling for one's own soil and people. When the people of one nation sincerely and strongly feel that their country is the best, that it is the bearer of the true culture and civilisation, the herald of all progress and liberty, then it is not an unjust procedure for them to try to force light and sweetness into other countries, whether they are willing or unwilling. We have the light, and others outside the country perish for want of it. It then becomes our duty to let them have light and obtain salvation. The progressive nations naturally feel that they are the elect of God and the Almighty has given them a right to enter by peaceful penetration if possible, or

[1] *After the War.* [2] Treitschke, *Politics*, i. p. 284.

forced attack if necessary, other people's houses to set them in order. Thus naturally and unconsciously, the spirit of nationalism results in forced conversion, aggressive expansion and predatory imperialism. "The civic, the feudal, or the oligarchic state passes into the national, the national into the imperial."[1] Attempts are made to force unwilling nations like the Poles, the Finns, and the Alsatians into absorption in nations of superior strength and numbers. Each man loves his country, and where there is increase of population closely pressing on the margin of subsistence, it is too much to think that he will devise measures other than extension of territory to satisfy his growing needs. A desire to get as much of the earth's surface as possible becomes the dominant motive. "All over the globe to-day we see the peoples of Europe creating a mighty aristocracy of the white races. Those who take no share in this great rivalry will play a pitiable part in time to come. The colonising impulse has become a vital question for a great nation." "Up to the present, Germany has always had too small a share of the spoils in

[1] Cramb, *The Origins and Destiny of Imperial Britain.*

the partition of non-European territories among the powers of Europe, and yet our existence as a state of the first rank is vitally affected by the question whether we can become a power beyond the seas."[1] While anxious to extend their dominions for self-aggrandisement, they do not publicly avow their purpose; they are not fools to flout the moral sense of the world. They take their stand on the highest ideals of humanity, and say they are out on the mission of civilising the backward races of the earth. If it is a sword which we see in the one hand to cut the way, the other hand will have the Bible to deceive the world. There is also the consideration of the great loss to humanity if large portions of the world are left undeveloped. If inferior races are not able to develop the resources of their regions, it becomes the duty of the higher and the more civilised to do it. This is nothing extraordinary, for it is the law written on every page of the book of nature, the law of the survival of the fittest. The more efficient should displace the less efficient. Thus the necessity to find room for the surplus popula-

[1] Treitschke, *Politics*, i. pp. 7 and 13.

tion, the civilising mission of the more evolved, the need for developing the unexploited portions of the earth's surface, and the vital faith in the higher purpose and destiny of one's own nation, all converge in imperialism.

Realpolitik, which has for its principle, "It is good when I steal your cow, and bad when you steal my cow," has been the governing force of European relations all these four or five centuries. Self-interest is the end; brute-force, the means; conscience is taboo. "In every part of the world, where British interests are at stake, I am in favour of advancing and upholding these interests, even at the cost of annexation and at the risk of war. The only qualification I admit is that the country we desire to annex, or take under our protection, the claims we choose to assert, and the cause we desire to espouse, should be calculated to confer a tangible advantage upon the British Empire."[1] Here we have an open

[1] Edward Dicey, "Peace and War," *Nineteenth Century*, September 1899. This quotation from a British writer is likely to mislead the reader into thinking that the imperialistic creed which is the logical outcome of the mechanical ideal is practised by Britain to the exclusion of higher considerations. But this suggestion is far from our intention. We give it as a definition of the low imperialistic creed and not as the policy of the British Empire. The imperialism which

avowal of the *Realpolitik* and a definition of the imperialist creed. Let your one aim be to extend the Empire; do not lift your little finger, unless by so doing, some tangible advantage is secured; if your material interests

---

holds extension of empire to be the sole aim, is not characteristic of the present time, at all events, of the British Empire. Seeley has taught us that the British Empire was acquired absent-mindedly, without any deliberate design, almost without effort at a time when colonies were easy to acquire. Now that Britain finds herself at the head of an Empire, she is trying to interpret her duty in a broad and liberal sense—we need not mind the croakers. She has not tried to impose her culture and civilisation on her dominions. The Prime Minister of England, Mr. Lloyd George, declared in a recent speech: "The idea that you cannot have many nations in the Empire is perishing of its own folly." Australia, Canada, New Zealand, etc., are free dominions; South Africa was granted self-government immediately after annexation; Home Rule for Ireland is on the Statute Book. Britain is determined to grant India ere long complete autonomy within the Empire, whatever vested interests might say. Empire in the sense of the federation of the free, is the ideal of Britain, and it has the hearty approval and sympathy of Rabindranath Tagore, as of all right-thinking men. Since writing the above, we have had definite statements from Messrs. Asquith and Lloyd George about the war aims of Britain. In an interview with Mr. Edward Marshall of the *Observer*, Mr. Asquith said: "The first thing needed is without doubt not a re-establishment of the balance of power but the removal of one of the chief of the chronic causes of unsettlement by the emancipation and regrouping of subject peoples in accordance with their aspirations and interests." He reiterated this view in his speech at Birmingham (December 1917), when he declared that "it is a root principle of democracy that every organised people is the true, the authentic, the final and the only responsible judge of its own form of government." Mr. Lloyd George, in his speech at Westminster on the 5th of January, emphasised that democratic principles should be applied not only in the settlement of the European questions but throughout the world. Judged by these utterances, it is clear that Britain does not intend to be imperialistic in the narrow sense of the term.

require annexation, war, and brutal treatment of other nations, do not scruple to adopt them.

The present War is the penalty which Europe pays for its steadfast loyalty to a false ideal. Selfish nationalism which despised the coloured races of the world is the root cause of this World War. The War is the logical result of the jealousy and rivalry among European nations who had all the one aim of using the backward peoples for their own selfish gain and interest.

On the seashore of the West
The funeral pyres are emitting
The last flames
Caught from the torch of a selfish, decadent civilisation.

The worship of energy
In the battlefield or factories
Is not worshipping thee,
The protector of the Universe.[1]

This imperialism is an elusive force which assumes different shapes. When we are in a mood to condemn it, we put it down for the expression of nationalist pride; when we wish to justify it, it becomes the only medium through which light and sweetness can be spread. Nationalism defeats itself if imperialism

[1] "The Blood-red Line," Rabindranath Tagore in the *Independent*.

is justified. Selfish nationalism has within it the seeds of its own destruction. Imperialism means nationalism or independence of the stronger and parasitism or subjection for the weaker. When we justify imperialism, that is, the substitution of the stronger for the weaker, we also justify wars. The races which are exploited will regard themselves as unjustly held in bondage, and will struggle to gain their independence. If they are strong like Germany and Italy in the nineteenth century, they throw off their yoke and attain freedom; if weak like Poland, or China at the present moment, they are trampled under foot. Empire is the enemy of nationality. It includes within it nations which, through lack of political genius or superiority of the conquering host, are controlled by an alien nation. These subject countries will always be a thorn in the side, unless they are treated in a spirit of liberal statesmanship. Empires can only be maintained by force. The task to establish world-unity by force and subjection has been essayed by many nations of the world—Egypt, Babylon, Persia, Greece, Rome, Spain, France, etc., but without success. Where these have failed no nation of the present day can hope to succeed.

Some people wrongly imagine that recasting the map of Europe on the principle of nationality would secure abiding peace. Rabindranath is clear that this is of no use. "You say these machines will come into an agreement, for their mutual protection, based upon a conspiracy of fear. But will this federation of steam-boilers supply you with a soul, a soul which has her conscience and her God? What is to happen to that larger part of the world where fear will have no hand in restraining you?"[1] Peace will not last long if it is based only on fear and weakness. For with a mechanical basis and a mechanical ideal, there is room in the world for one nation, and peace will not break out until that end is attained. The system proceeds on the view that the gain of one nation is the loss of another. Until the material basis and aim are removed there will be wars and fresh wars till the world gets cold and the last man sinks into sleep, wars bred by territorial acquisition in tropical regions, commercial exploitation

[1] *Nationalism.*

and desire to possess exclusive markets. When the freed European nations stand up face to face with their full individualities developed, their one interest will be to push onward and upward and get as much as possible of the non-European world. So long as there is one dark spot on earth, unpossessed by European nations, all eyes will be turned to it and inevitably there will be a conflict among the competitors. The earth is neither unlimited nor its wealth boundless to satisfy all the nations of Europe for all time. Supposing the whole world is parcelled out among the powers, even then wars will not cease. If another planet does not drop at the feet of Europe to keep it engaged, the overlordship of the universe will be contested. In this race only one nation can be at the top, and all European powers will struggle to gain that top place. No one can hope to have an easy climb up, for the European nations trained in militarist methods, unless they are crushed beyond the possibility of revival, will not allow one of themselves to steal a march over others. They will devise a delicate balance of power which even small differences will upset. If imperialism at any time can give us peace it is only after the whole world has passed under the domination of one single nation, for it requires at least two to make a quarrel. This consummation of a single world-power will not occur before the world is converted into a charnel-house and collapses into a heap of dust. Professor Cramb says: "In the light of history, universal peace appears less as a dream than as a nightmare which shall be realised only when the ice has crept into the heart of the sun, and the stars, left black and trackless, start from their orbits."[1] To the same effect, Treitschke: "War will endure to the end of history. The laws of human thought and of human nature forbid any alternative, neither is one to be wished for."[2] Nationality becomes a curse; it separates nations from one another. Neither love nor idealism governs their relations: fear and jealousy develop. Nations acquire faith in armaments and navies, aeroplanes and Krupp guns. In countries where the political civilisation prevails nations "live in an atmosphere of fear, greed,

[1] *The Origin and Destiny of Imperial Britain.*

[2] *Politics*, i. p. 65.

and panic, due to the preying of one nation upon other for material wealth. Its civilisation is carnivorous and cannibalistic, feeding upon the blood of weaker nations. Its one idea is to thwart all greatness outside its own boundaries. Never before were there such terrible jealousies, such betrayals of trust; all this is called patriotism, whose creed is politics."[1] Millions of human beings have been the victims of this false idol. The sacrifice of body and the torture of heart, the wastage of spirit and the wreckage of soul occasioned by the worship of this idol are appalling. Highly civilised Europe does not feel the odium of its policy, for it is accustomed to traditions of conquest and exploitation. It is the air it breathes, and therefore it does not stupefy. But outsiders feel the poison. Unless the gospel of imperialism which cuts athwart the fundamentals of democracy and humanity is laid to rest for all time, there is no hope for the world. If the spirit of nationalism is not ended, we shall soon have an end of nations. Any tinkering with this clear goal will dash to pieces the hope of humanity and cause a

[1] *Nationalism.*

repetition of all this madness. The truth about nationalism, viz.: rule with the consent of the governed, should be extended to the non-European countries. At the present day the principle of nationality recognises the barriers of race and colour; but until these adventitious barriers are broken down, there is no chance of permanent peace. Democracy asserts that, not only man must not be exploited by man, but also that nation must not be allowed to exploit nation. What Europe has come to believe to be necessary for the individual's highest self-development, should also be affirmed of nations; for to Rabindranath, personality is found in peoples as well as in individuals. "The peoples are living beings having their distinct personalities."[1] They have their own soul and genius which should be allowed to express itself and develop freely and fully. We should recognise personality wherever it is, in weaker nations or stronger ones. Failure to recognise this led to the War. The States are in a diseased or disorganised condition, and wars are the external symptoms of this disease. Plato argues rightly that wars break

[1] "The Nation," *Modern Review*, July 17, p. 1.

out when the States become internally diseased. The more they are distracted within, the more they come into conflict without. The present disease of the European States is their subjection to the mechanical idea, and they show their sickness of soul by oppressing subject races and small nationalities, creating resentments and encouraging oppressions. They show it by their ambition and vanity, self-glory and love of land. An ideal state will be against war. It will have for its goal, not the nation, but the people of the Eastern world. In his lectures on "Nationalism" Rabindranath draws a distinction between "nation" and "people," and considers that nation is the modern Western type, and people the ancient Eastern ideal. A nation, as it is now interpreted in the West, has become a terrible machine, killing all others, using all science for its end, and ultimately making a whole people lose their higher ideals, and serve only in the interests of the State. Rabindranath defines a nation as "an organised gregariousness of gluttony." It is a machine dead and soulless, making the human units who form parts of it lose their life and soul, and become lifeless units of a dead machine.

But a people is a living soul. It is spiritual and alive. The peoples of the East do not organise themselves for power but for perfection. They do not hate and kill, suspect and envy, but live and adore, love and worship. The individuals of a nation do things like a machine, while those of a people have the elasticity of life and flexibility of soul. Eastern nations are still peoples, though they are slowly losing that character, captured by the glamour of the West. "Japan too was a people. But the West in the voice of her thundering cannon had said at the door of Japan, Let there be a nation, and there was a nation. And now that it has come into existence, why do you not feel in your heart of hearts a pure feeling of gladness and say that it is good? The same vices which seem so natural and innocuous in its own life make it surprised and angry at their unpleasantness when seen in other nations. Therefore when you see the Japanese nation, created in your own image, launched in its career of national boastfulness, you shake your head and say it is not good."[1] "We realise in our sober moments that it is not good to

[1] *Nationalism*, pp. 39-48.

develop the national spirit, and yet we have no respect for the no-nations of the world."[1] Europe never cared for Japan when she was a people. But now she is ever anxious to please her and treat her with all consideration. "Japan had all her wealth of humanity, her harmony of heroism and beauty, her depth of self-control and richness of self-expression; yet the Western nations felt no respect for her till she proved that the bloodhounds of Satan are not only bred in the kennels of Europe, but can also be domesticated in Japan, and fed with man's miseries."[2] If Europe can reach the Eastern ideal of a people she will have a future more glorious than her past.

IV

Rabindranath is not without hope for the future of Europe. He knows that from time to time have risen in Europe "noble minds who have ever stood up for the rights of man, irrespective of colour and creed, who have braved calumny and insult from their own

[1] "The Nation," *Modern Review*, July 17.
[2] *Nationalism*, p. 83.

people in fighting for humanity's cause and raising their voices against the mad orgies of militarism. These are there to prove that the fountain-head of the water of everlasting life has not run dry in Europe, and from thence she will have her rebirth time after time."[1] Optimist that he is, Rabindranath believes that war is not only destructive but also creative, and hopes that the present war convulsions will usher in a new era, setting free the human spirit which has been striving for voice and utterance all these years. This bath of blood will wipe off all dross and impurity; and this martyrdom will be the path which will lead Europe back to the heaven of love. Men passing through this hell will learn to love heaven better. Suffering by making egoisms vanish and purifying desires will fuse the different individuals into one soul. The little idol self will be broken. The breath of heaven will blow and will shatter it to bits. Small egoisms will be caught up in the splendour of sacrifice; man will have his rebirth. An abiding faith in spirit will be the net result of this War. Faith born in a great crisis is a

[1] *Nationalism*, p. 66.

fresh discovery. In the thunder of guns and clash of armies, in the shrieks of hatred and the groans of death, in the cries of woe and the wailings of despair, the poet hears the clear, though terrible voice of God, chastising the followers of a material civilisation and pointing out to them that when logically followed out, that civilisation would make it hard to live the life of a human being on this planet. It is hoped that those who have seen the face of death, when they return, will disinfect the nations of all poison of materialism.

> Shall the value of the martyrs' blood and mothers' tears be utterly lost in the dust of the earth, not buying Heaven with their price?
> And when Man bursts his mortal bounds, is not the Boundless revealed that moment?[1]

The chance for Europe after the War lies in her adoption of the ideals of the East, namely spiritual love, beauty, and freedom, which are not diminished by sharing.

> I sat alone in a corner of my house, thinking it too narrow for any guest, but now when its door is flung open by an unbidden joy I find there is room for thee and for all the world.[2]

---

[1] *Fruit-Gathering*, LXXXIV. [2] *Ibid.* LXXVI.

India, which may be taken as a typical representative of the East, never went out on an adventure of commerce and conquest. It was her proud privilege to be the fountain source of the ideals of beauty, truth, and love, and wholesome living. The West if it seeks salvation should take to these Eastern ideals of spirit.

> Yes, the rays of thy light and joy are lying latent in the East to liberate the soul of the world.[1]

The change of heart necessary for the reconstruction of the world on a spiritual basis is possible in the present crisis, when all are disgusted with the cruelties of war. It is possible that human nature may now purge itself of all its cunning and cupidity, sloth and selfishness. The tribal Gods of practice already slain in philosophy and theology will be slain in life and politics. The queer spectacle of the Church running after the State and justifying everything the State proposes to do, will become a thing of the past. The one God of religion and philosophy, instead of being a theme of academic discussion, will become the living faith of mankind. Chris-

[1] "The Blood-red Line," in the *Independent*.

tianity is the enemy of selfish nationalism and imperialism, as all true religion is. Its greatest contribution to the growth of freedom is its insistence on the incalculable value of human personality. When the conscience of the world, hypnotised by its own past, was revelling in its slavery and forgot the sacred mystery of human nature, Christianity appeared on the scene, emphatically declaring the worth of the individual. Christianity believed in democracy, not merely that men should be equal but nations. Democracy insists on the rights of all nations to equal freedom, as every nation has a right to be itself. So Christianity sternly rebuked the policy of expansion. "Thou shalt not covet thy neighbour's land. Thou shalt not covet thy neighbour's sea, nor his forts, nor his ports, nor his shops, nor his ships, nor anything that is his." The world is wide enough for all nations to live peaceably together, if only they give up their ideas of racial pride and animosity. The Universe is to be viewed as a single family where the different nations are the members, each contributing its quota to the welfare of the whole. All peoples will then have a place in the sun. In Rabindranath's image: "As the mission of the rose lies in the unfoldment of the petals which implies distinctness, so the rose of humanity is perfect only when the diverse races and the nations have evolved their perfected distinct characteristics but all attached to the stem of humanity by the bond of love." Nations should preserve their identity, for each nation has a right to its expression as a part of the whole. He does not think that this preservation of the national soul of each unit would work against the brotherhood of man. A dead level of mechanical monotony and dull uniformity which would reduce all nations and races to one type is undesirable, and should be replaced by a spiritual whole of varied aspects and beauty. Each type of culture must bring its own contribution to the world. A vague cosmopolitanism is of no good. "We shall realise that only through the development of racial individuality can we truly attain to universality, and only in the light of the spirit of universality can we perfect individualty."[1] Rabindranath advocates the ideal of unity and harmony, and not uniformity

[1] *My Interpretation of Indian History.*

and identity, for the latter aim, if achieved, would rob life of all charm and incident and enthrone a dull monotony of ideas and aims. Besides, the ideal of melting all races into one mould is against the nature of things and cannot be achieved. Rabindranath puts forward a plea for mankind by advocating the ideal of a family of nations to which every member will bring his unique gift. This ideal international unity and national independence will break down the barriers of nations and make for sweet harmony. Then will civilisations be inspired by the ideas of the wholeness of the world and its oneness. Then shall we know that there is no such thing as the over-lordship of the universe. There is no pre-eminence of any one nation in everything. If one nation is the first politically, another will be so religiously, a third in art, and so on. All are equally great and equally necessary for the music of life and the harmony of the universe. The beauty of this variegated world requires the free and independent existence of all nations. All nations are sacred to themselves and to each other, because they are sacred to the whole. Each contributes to the wealth of the universe and derives from it. There is no need for one nation to fight the others out of existence. Only this gift of freedom and independence to all the nations of the world can put a stop to the long-standing feuds of races and nations. The lost faith in the brotherhood of nations would be recovered. Instead of being the poet's dream, it would become a living force. Then will the world be transformed into an Empire of the free, or an International Commonwealth based on disinterested and self-sacrificing nationalism. As morality, in individual relations, means the subordination of the individual inclinations to the law of duty, so international morality means the subordination of the selfish advantages of nations to the claims of humanity and the world at large. Selfishness is sin whether in individuals or in nations. It is immoral to think that moral principles have no place in politics. They are for outside use as much as for home consumption. The State represents the general will of the community. Truth and honour are as sacred to it as to individuals. The State is not an end in itself. It is not higher than the moral law. When this reversal of values takes place then the better minds of nations will repudiate war as the failure of reason and abdication of spirit. From this holocaust real spiritual democracy may be born. The belligerent peoples are in a mood of self-examination. The note of interrogation meets us everywhere. It is seriously asked, Have we lived the religion of brotherhood to which we have intellectually assented? It is the unique privilege of the present generation of men to organise a spiritual democracy which will embrace the whole of humanity, and set up a central power to enforce international security. Till such a world-concert, based on unselfishness and respect for human life of any creed or race, is established, Hague Palaces, Leagues of Peace, and Councils of Conciliation will be ineffective.

V

When Rabindranath condemned the selfish nationalist spirit of the West in strong terms, he was asked with what logic he could denounce the principle of nationalism, when, for the lack of it, India is lying down humble and humiliated as a "defeated and conquered nation." He answered that the dust in which India's people have been bowed is more sacred than the bricks which build the palaces of our temporal pride and power, for "this dust is fertile of life, and of beauty and worship."

> Those who walk on the path of pride crushing the lowly life under their tread, covering the tender green of the earth with their footprints in blood;
>
> Let them rejoice, and thank thee, Lord, for the day is theirs.
>
> But I am thankful that my lot lies with the humble who will suffer and bear the burden of power, and hide their faces and stifle their sobs in the dark.
>
> For every throb of their pain has pulsed in the secret depth of thy night, and every insult has been gathered into the great silence.
>
> And the morrow is theirs.
>
> O Sun, rise upon the bleeding hearts blossoming in flowers of the morning, and the torchlight revelry of pride shrunken to ashes.[1]

Rabindranath exhorts the Indians not to be ashamed of their condition but be of good cheer.

> Be not ashamed, my Brothers, to stand before the proud and the powerful with your white robe of simpleness.
>
> Let your crown be of humility, your freedom the freedom of the soul.

---

[1] *Fruit-Gathering*, LXXXVI.

Build God's throne daily upon the ample bareness of your poverty.

And know what is huge is not great and pride is not everlasting.[1]

VI

Rabindranath is a nationalist, but not of the wrong type. While he loves his country, he does not hate others. His patriotism is quite compatible with universal love. While national independence is a phase of social evolution to be necessarily passed through, it is ultimately one to be transcended in the conception of a world-whole. As each nation embodies some peculiar elements of value necessary for the full expression of Man, the love of a nation as embodying a part of the essence is not incompatible with the love of mankind as a whole. When Rabindranath wants India to build a great future it is not on the national basis. He wants India to attain freedom that she might make her contribution to the world's welfare, that she might be in a position to fulfil her destiny and carry her message through the world. When Rabindranath loves India, it is the love of a soul,

[1] *The Sunset of the Century.*

of a spiritual principle and not that of land or commerce. He does not want India to struggle for the sake of her national resources, for preserving the integrity of her forests, saving her mines from destruction and keeping the physical wealth of the great country for the use of her posterity. To him this is a low ideal. No doubt it is a great waste from the Indian point of view that India's material resources are exploited by other countries. But this—a few millions more or less—is not a great thing. When the professional politician complains that foreign rule is bad because wealth emigrates, taxation increases, industries diminish, and hundreds of thousands of people perish in famines, it does not appeal to him as forcibly as considerations of soul and culture. The soul of the Indian nation, its ideal, its thought, its conscience, is at stake, the soul with all its aspirations towards the just and the true, with all that constitutes the human being. His point is that national culture dwindles, soul is subdued, and everything that makes a nation great, faith, purpose, and character, is inevitably melting away. It is the yoke of the mind, the disease of the soul that he points his finger at. We are steadily losing the ancient culture of India, "the culture that enjoins man to look for his true wealth and power in his inner soul, the culture that gives self-possession in the face of loss and danger, self-sacrifice without counting the cost or hoping for gain, defiance of death, acceptance of countless social obligations that we owe to men as social beings."[1] This, according to him, is a measure of our loss and the extent of our ruin. Spiritual powers and resources of India are being wasted; the diviner human powers of feeling and imagination which reach to the inmost depth of being are neither touched nor developed. In the process of secularisation of life, immense potential resources of spiritual wealth are being lost. The way to grow is by keeping the spiritual achievements of the race in the past before the eyes of the present, by preserving the priceless treasures of mind and soul and by incorporating the great spiritual inheritance in the lives of India's present and future citizens. We need to find ways to make available our choicest racial possessions and bring them to bear upon the

[1] *Nationalism*, p. 53.

lives of the many. It is the spiritual ideal of India that will lend freedom to the human spirit, and break the bonds of narrow and cramping environment. We must war against the rising tendency for the soul to be swallowed up by mere things, that we might get back the mystic sense of communion with the divine.

> Thou hast given us to live,
> Let us uphold this honour with all our strength and will;
> For Thy glory rests upon the glory that we are.
> Therefore in Thy name we oppose the power that would plant its banner upon our soul.[1]

India should have freedom to express her soul with its longing for holiness, its joy of adoration, its fierce spiritual questioning, and its flaming passion for righteousness. Political freedom is not an end in itself. It is a means to the higher freedom of soul. India should be allowed to solve her problems according to her national genius. It is not because India guards under her soil the bones of our fathers, but because she stands for an eternal principle —that life is a spiritual aspiration, matter the handiwork of spirit, and all universe one in spirit. This ought to inspire and govern all

[1] *India's Prayer.*

efforts. To the people of India India's immortal soul has stood between the human race and its sinful and savage instincts. But under the impulse of the West, Indians are exchanging their spiritual wealth for the latest scraps of knowledge. They are losing their high standards of courage and courtesy, fair play and holiness, dreamed and achieved in the past. Belief in life immortal, belief in holiness, austerity, and the resolute turning away from all shams and mere outward appearances to the souls of things, and belief in the vision which saw that body was naught and spirit all, are dying away. So Rabindranath asks us to win freedom in the name of the spirit and fight for the lost provinces of the soul. "The wakeful ageless God of India calls to-day on our soul—the soul that is measureless, the soul that is undefeated, the soul that is destined to immortality, and yet the soul which lies to-day in the dust, humbled by external authority, in the fetters of blind observances. With blow upon blow, pang upon pang, does He call upon it 'Atmanam Viddhi,' know thyself."[1] All the world over the spirit of

[1] *Modern Review*, September 1917, p. 339.

freedom is awake. But where is India? Can she alone remain immune from its contagion? Can she alone remain unshaken by a passion which is so universal in its power over men? Rise, India! Break up the spell of old tradition, cut off the meshes of despotism and return to the ancient though despised ideals of spirit and liberty.

The day is come
But where is India?
Strike thy blow at her self-suspicion and despair.
Save her from the dread of her pursuing shadow, O Lord,
ever awake.[1]

Rabindranath does not want India to worship efficiency and machinery and build her fabric on fear and discipline, but wishes her to practise the love that gives but does not grasp, and build on the stable foundations of freedom and goodwill. Regaining faith in her own soul, and the "soul whose revelation is the world," India shall guard herself against automatism, keep life free and creative, and proceed from creation to creation in an unending flow.

1 "The Day is come," *Modern Review*, September 17, p. 231.